Praise for

THE CYNIC

"While MacGillis writes with the passion of a convert, he isn't some liberal hack whom Republicans can coolly dismiss. He is a thorough and well-trained reporter happily unburdened from the dispassionate constraints of he-said-she-said journalism. . . . In *The Cynic,* MacGillis constructs his profile around interviews with long-lost friends, colleagues and enemies—more than 75 of them for this slim volume—who have known the subject since their provincial early days."

—*The Washington Post*

"The best portrait of McConnell."

—NationalJournal.com

"Not many people have a clear idea of who McConnell is, or how he evolved, or why he does the things he does. . . . This is the story Alec MacGillis tells in his concise, fast-moving [book] about McConnell, *The Cynic.* It's full of things I hadn't known. . . . He also helps explain how someone without the obvious political gifts of speechmaking or glad-handing has stayed in national office for 30 years and is favored to be there at least six years more. And if you'd like even more firsthand evidence of what has happened to the Senate, you'll find it here—all in less than two hours' reading time."

—James Fallows

"MacGillis's book serves as a great reminder of how McConnell became the Senate leader he is today—and how much every elected official tends to change the more they learn about Washington and their polarized constituents."

—TheWashingtonPost.com

"As Alec MacGillis's excellent new book on McConnell makes clear, the Kentucky senator's top priority has always been not ideology but his own political advancement and survival."

—TheAtlantic.com

THE CYNIC

The Political Education of Mitch McConnell

ALEC MACGILLIS

Simon & Schuster Paperbacks

New York   London   Toronto   Sydney   New Delhi

Simon & Schuster Paperbacks
A Division of Simon & Schuster, Inc.
1230 Avenue of the Americas
New York, NY 10020

First Simon & Schuster trade paperback edition December 2014

SIMON & SCHUSTER PAPERBACKS and colophon are registered
trademarks of Simon & Schuster, Inc.

The Simon & Schuster Speakers Bureau can bring authors
to your live event. For more information or to book an event contact
the Simon & Schuster Speakers Bureau at 1-866-248-3049 or visit
our website at www.simonspeakers.com.

Interior design by Lewelin Polanco

Manufactured in the United States of America

ISBN 978-1-5011-1203-4 (pbk)
ISBN 978-1-4767-6107-7 (ebook)

CONTENTS

A NOTE ON SOURCES

The Cynic is based on interviews with more than seventy-five people who have worked alongside Mitch McConnell or otherwise interacted with him over the course of his career. McConnell declined to be interviewed, as did his wife, Elaine Chao. Many of the McConnell remarks and observations quoted in the book are derived from John David Dyche's authorized 2009 biography of McConnell, *Republican Leader*. Dyche interviewed McConnell for his book and also was granted access to oral history interviews that McConnell gave over the years to John Kleber, a Kentucky historian. Other books helpful in researching this book include Geoffrey Kabaservice's *Rule and Ruin*, Robert A. Caro's *Master of the Senate*, Gabriel Sherman's *The Loudest Voice in the Room,* and Norman Ornstein and Thomas Mann's *It's Even Worse Than It Looks*. Among the many articles that informed the book were Clara Bingham's 2005 piece in *Washington Monthly* on the Martin County slurry spill, Phillip Babich's 2003 piece on the same subject in *Salon*, John Judis's 2001 piece in the *New Republic* on McConnell's relations with China, John Cheves's 2006 series in the *Lexington Herald-Leader* on McConnell's interactions with campaign donors, Joshua Green's 2011 profile of McConnell in the *Atlantic*, and Jason Cherkis and Zach Carter's 2013 profile of him in *The Huffington Post*. The book is also indebted to the daily beat reporting of Capitol Hill veterans such as the *Washington Post*'s Paul Kane, the *New York Times*' Carl Hulse, and the *Louisville Courier-Journal*'s James R. Carroll, among others.

The author made two reporting trips to Kentucky in the course of researching the book, to western Kentucky in August 2013 and Louisville and eastern Kentucky in April 2014.

THE CYNIC

PREFACE

The young man seemed hopeless. He was an underwhelming specimen, with a wan complexion, thin lips, and doughy features, as well as a slight limp, the legacy of a childhood bout with polio. "Doesn't make a dominant physical presentation," was how the pollster, Tully Plesser, put it years later. "He wasn't like a man's man, really," said the ad maker, Bob Goodman. The candidate was even less commanding in his speech, with none of the rhetorical vigor expected of politicians in Appalachia and the upland South. And he offered precious little material for the image shapers: the son of a middle manager, not even a native of the state in which he was running for office, with nothing in his background but a few years of low-level lawyering and Washington paper-shuffling. "He isn't interesting. He doesn't have an aura, an air of mystery about him," said Goodman, the man charged with conjuring something out of these paltry fixings.

Yet in another light, Addison Mitchell McConnell Jr. was an ideal project. For one, he was unburdened by any illusions about his shortcomings.

For another, he wanted to win.

And so the young man submitted to the consultants' instructions like no candidate they had known. "He was wonderful," said Goodman. "He was like a kid doing a new thing. He was very easy to deal with. He was like the kid who never was in the school play, who really didn't have talent that way, but was very willing to do the things asked of him." Said Plesser: "We didn't have to deal with the ego. Mitch was the best client to have. He really listened, he didn't argue. . . . We were absolutely starting from scratch. We could build something just the way we wanted, with no pushback." And when the candidate proceeded to exceed the low expectations others had for him—finally nailing the clip on the seventh or eighth take—he glowed with gratification, said Goodman: "He appreciated a compliment: 'You did that great!' It was like the kid who says, 'Gosh, I really *can* do the school play.'" One of the guys on the film crew came up with a behind-his-back nickname for the eager striver: *"Love-me-love-me."*

The challenge was obvious, said Goodman. "Being dramatic was not his style. We saw it as his weakness as a politician and we said, 'How do we take this fellow who doesn't do all the political things and endear him to a constituency that just wants to talk common sense? How do we lighten him up and make him human, reach the human feelings of hope and love?' He was open to that, because he recognized that wasn't his strength."

The consultants did their job, and their man won, narrowly defeating the incumbent Democrat to become, in 1978, the head of government for Jefferson County, Kentucky, which includes Louisville. To their astonishment, he did not stop there. This man so ill-suited to the business of running for elected office went on to knock off an incumbent U.S. senator in 1984, becoming the first Republican to win statewide in Kentucky in sixteen years, and then to win reelection four times, and then to find himself in 2014 on the verge of achieving what fairly early in his ascent he had identified as his life's dream: Senate majority leader.

But it was not just their former client's climb up the ladder that startled the consultants. It was the way his ascent transformed him. The guileless young man who was conspicuously uninformed about the mechanics of politics grew into a steely influence broker, proud of his growing sway on Capitol Hill. More than that, what struck Goodman was how his former client was using that power—to obstruct the agenda of President Barack Obama and, with it, the workings of the federal government. The young man who had run in Louisville as a pragmatic moderate—who had won the endorsement

of the AFL-CIO by supporting collective bargaining for public employees, who had earned the gratitude of local feminists by standing
up for abortion rights—was now the symbol of the willful intran-
sigence that had brought the nation's capital to the brink of utter
dysfunction. And this change pained Bob Goodman.

"It's so sad and disillusioning to me," said Goodman. "I guess
it's part of his pragmatism: it was his strategy to say no to Obama
on everything. It obviously works. But it works to the detriment of
the country. I hate it. I hate the fact that he was right there." Goodman pores over the recollections of his years working with McConnell but can find no premonitions of what came later. "There were
no alarm bells coming out of him," he said. "He was a perfectly
reasonable guy."

There is an understandable inclination to tell political history
through its most colorful characters—Teddy Roosevelt, LBJ, Bill
Clinton. But our times are often shaped as much, if not more, by
our more nondescript figures. To understand what has happened
in Washington over the past few decades, as our government has
become increasingly incapable of tackling the problems of our
times—sluggish wages, a broken immigration system, and climate
change, to name just a few—we must seek to understand Mitch
McConnell. It is he who symbolizes better than anyone else in
politics today the transformation of the Republican Party from a
broad, nationwide coalition spanning conservatives, moderates,
and even some liberals into an ideologically monolithic, demo-
graphically constrained unit that political scientists judge without
modern historical precedence.

But the story of Mitch McConnell is about more than ideology.
It is about character. For under that inexpressive visage that Goodman and Plesser sought to break through, there lies a morality tale
that goes to the heart of our country's political culture—and the
weakness within it.

Chapter One

RUN, RUN, RUN

McConnell's youth was peripatetic—his early years were spent in Athens, Alabama, a small town in the northern end of the state; at eight his family moved to Augusta, Georgia; and before the start of high school they arrived in Louisville, where his father, a manager with DuPont, had been transferred. His parents hailed mostly from Scots-Irish stock, more humble on his mother's side (tenant farmers) than on his father's (his lineage included a county judge and mortician).

From age two to four, McConnell suffered from polio, and his mother, who was named Julia but went by Dean, devoted herself to the rehabilitation of her only child. She brought him to the polio treatment retreat founded by Franklin D. Roosevelt in Warm Springs, Georgia, but there were no rooms available, so staff instead instructed her on how to do the physical therapy back home on her own, with occasional visits to Warm Springs to check on Mitch's progress. And she *was* on her own—her husband was with the army in Europe in the final months of World War II. There were three hours of exercises to be done each day, and Dean was under orders to keep Mitch off his partially paralyzed left leg, so coming and going meant carrying the boy up and down the stairs of their walk-up apartment building. When he was deemed recovered, his mother bought him low-top saddle oxfords. "That seems like such a small thing, but to me, it was huge," he said later. "Now I was just like every other kid."

In later years, McConnell often pointed to his recovery from polio as the foundational event in his life, a declaration often paired with an expression of "a great deal of gratitude toward his mother," says Meme Sweets Runyon, who worked for McConnell in his first campaign and elected office. His parents' approach to that battle, he'd tell people, turned him into a person who "liked to solve problems." "His parents were very organized and methodical. They had that methodical way of addressing a problem," says Runyon. It also explained his determination. "It taught him that you can get through a really crippling situation—literally—by putting one step in front of the other," Runyon says. Charles Musson, a Louisville lawyer who also worked on McConnell's first campaign, was blunter: "It made him a fighter," he says.

In what realm to fight and strive? Young Mitch loved sports, but while he did manage to play baseball with his slight limp, dreams of sports stardom were out. (A meticulously detailed score sheet he kept at age thirteen shows him with a .295 regular season batting average but an .074 playoff one.) Instead, in high school McConnell gravitated to that other realm favored by competitive young American men with a head for stats: politics. He was a serious history buff, steeped in the lore of great Kentucky statesmen such as Henry Clay, and at age fourteen he watched every minute of coverage of both party's 1956 conventions. It was easy to imagine him growing up to be part of the political support staff that would soon dominate Washington, the pundits and aides and strategists who can recite election results from decades past and who advise the candidate out front on what to say and how to vote. It was harder to imagine McConnell as the front man himself, what with his blinking bearing and introverted nature.

But young Mitch wanted to be a candidate after all. Runyon points to a simple explanation: "Mitch is an only child. Only children love attention." He was introverted, but not so shy that he disliked the spotlight. Shortly after arriving in Louisville, by far the largest city he'd ever lived in, McConnell became vice president of the junior high student council. At duPont Manual High School, he set about improving on that rank and by junior year managed to win election as student body president, with a methodical effort that included stuffing pamphlets into each locker, even those belonging to students in the lower grades whom upperclassmen candidates often looked past. One pamphlet announced his endorsements from, among others, "the fastest halfback in the city" and "the president of the key club." At the University of Louisville, which he chose to attend to spare himself another move and stay close to Dean, the mother with whom he was so close, he kept on running—for freshman class president, for president of the student senate, for president of the student council of the College of Arts and Sciences. He lost all three, and took it hard despite the low stakes, as depicted in *Republican Leader,* a 2009 authorized biography of McConnell by John David Dyche. "McConnell realized that he had not worked as hard as he should have, and vowed to never make that mistake again," writes Dyche, a Louisville lawyer and conservative commentator. Once again, vindication arrived in junior year: he won the presidency of the student council.

It was time to get into politics for real. There was no question which party McConnell would associate himself with—the Democrats' Solid South had started splintering, and he'd had a sentimental attachment to the Republicans from a young age, largely out of loyalty to Dwight Eisenhower, the general who'd led his father in Europe. (In his third-grade class photo, Mitch wears an "I Like Ike" button.) And in Kentucky, Republicans were ascendant—the state went for Richard Nixon in 1960 (McConnell slapped a Nixon bumper sticker on the family car) and two well-regarded Republican senators represented the state.

The real question was not which party Mitch McConnell would sign up for. It was which kind of Republican he'd be.

It is nothing short of astonishing to contemplate just how ideologically diverse the Republican Party was a half century ago. Coming out of the relative stasis of the Eisenhower years, the party was in a free-for-all, with a new wave of combative conservatives, many of them hailing from the boomtowns of the Sun Belt, challenging the party's old-guard Midwestern centrists and conservatives and its Northeastern liberals. The dividing line in the mid-1960s was Lyndon B. Johnson's civil rights legislation, which passed with the staunch support of old-guard Republicans (17 of Ohio's 18 congressional Republicans backed the bill, notes Geoffrey Kabaservice in his 2012 history of moderate Republicanism, *Rule and Ruin*), even as many of the new-wave conservatives opposed it. The showdown came at the 1964 Republican National Convention, held at the Cow Palace in San Francisco, where Nelson Rockefeller was jeered to the point of inaudibility as he spoke in favor of a platform plank against extremists groups like the Ku Klux Klan and the John Birch Society. The convention ended with the nomination of Arizona senator Barry Goldwater, who had voted against the Civil Rights Act, passed earlier that year, and who punctuated his acceptance speech with a line that became the rallying cry for this new brand of conservatism: "I would remind you that extremism in the defense of liberty is no vice. And let me remind you also that moderation in the pursuit of justice is no virtue."

Back in Kentucky, Mitch McConnell had before him vivid representatives of both of the widely disparate poles of his party, and, like any young person finding his way, he sampled both. Under the influence of a conservative political science professor, McConnell invited Goldwater to campus, where McConnell introduced his speech. In the summer of 1963, he headed to Washington to intern for Gene Snyder, a highly conservative rookie congressman from Kentucky who warned of "creeping socialism" afoot in the land. McConnell was in Snyder's office for the March on Washington by

Rev. Martin Luther King Jr. and other civil rights leaders, but he couldn't show his excitement, not in front of Snyder—he slipped out on the steps of the Capitol to take in the crowds, but dared venture no further than that.

McConnell's desire to be out on the Mall for King's speech suggested the Goldwater wing of the party was not for him. Instead, he latched onto a more suitable model. Both of Kentucky's senators were well to the left of Snyder. It was Thruston Morton who would unsuccessfully try to gavel into silence the jeering crowd at the Cow Palace so that Rockefeller could be heard. And it was John Sherman Cooper who, far more than anyone, would shape the Republicanism of young Mitch.

Cooper was a remarkable figure, a patrician Yalie who had quit Harvard Law School on learning that his family's fortune had been wiped out by the recession of 1920 and had returned home to sell the family mansion, settle his father's debts, and set about putting his six siblings through college. He won a Bronze Star for his work rebuilding the Bavarian judicial system at the end of World War II and served as a special assistant to Secretary of State Dean Acheson during the creation of NATO. Arriving in Washington, he was one of the first Republicans to speak out against fellow Republican Joe McCarthy, and he voted with his party barely half the time. He became close friends with John F. Kennedy, a regular guest at the famous Georgetown soirees hosted by *Washington Post* publisher Katharine Graham, and an ardent opponent of the Vietnam War, joining with Idaho Democrat Frank Church to draft an amendment barring further action in Cambodia. He might well have run for higher office were it not for one shortcoming: he was, in his own words, "a truly terrible public speaker."

In 1964, that year of turmoil and soul-searching for the Grand Old Party, Cooper became Mitch McConnell's lodestar. After returning to Louisville in the fall of 1963, out from under Snyder's baleful eye, McConnell fired off a column urging Republicans to get on board with strong civil rights legislation at the state and national levels. Brimming with earnest idealism, the piece anticipates the main argument against civil rights reform and demolishes it: "Property rights have always been, and will continue to be, an integral part of our heritage, but this does not absolve the property holder of his obligation to help ensure the basic rights of all citizens." McConnell disputed the opposition's claim to constitutional rationales against the legislation: "One must view the Constitution as a document adaptable to conditions of contemporary society," he wrote, and any "strict interpretation" was "innately evil" if its result was that "basic rights are denied to any group."

By early spring, McConnell was speaking in a racially mixed assemblage at a campus "Freedom Rally" urging others to join King in marching on the state capital. As the divisive GOP presidential primary of that year took shape, McConnell sided against Goldwater and for two moderates—first Pennsylvania governor William Scranton and then ambassador to Vietnam Henry Cabot Lodge Jr. And at the end of the school year he was back in Washington, interning for the representative who was by this time the right fit: Cooper. That June, Cooper played a lead role in finagling just enough Republican votes to help break the filibuster of the Civil Rights Act led by Southern Democrats. And a year later, when McConnell was in Washington for a visit, Cooper brought him along to witness the signing of the Voting Rights Act.

Looking back, McConnell repeatedly cited Cooper's leadership on civil rights legislation, despite hailing from a Civil War border state, as his model for being a senator. He recounted asking Cooper at the time, "How do you take such a tough stand and square it with the fact that a considerable number of people who have chosen you have the opposite view?" To which, he says, Cooper responded: "I not only represent Kentucky, I represent the nation, and there are times when you follow, and there are times when you lead." McConnell expanded on this in his interviews with Dyche and in the annual oral history interviews McConnell has been giving for years to Kentucky historian John Kleber, which McConnell made available to Dyche. Cooper, he said, had often put him in mind of Edmund Burke's famous dictum: "Your representative owes, not his industry only, but his judgment, and betrays, instead of serving you, if he sacrifices it to your opinion." Cooper, McConnell said, "always carried out his best judgment instead of pandering to the popular view." He "was sensitive to what his constituents were interested in, but not controlled by it."

And Cooper showed that a senator with such independence of mind, forthrightness, and conviction could flourish. In 1966, he was reelected with nearly two-thirds of the vote.

———

As riveted as McConnell was by the civil rights battles in Washington, it was the other great issue of the 1960s that threatened a more personal impact. And on this score, he again followed Cooper's lead. In the fall of 1964, McConnell enrolled in law school at the University of Kentucky (thus allowing him to later claim both of the state's major colleges as alma maters). There, like many other students, he grew opposed to the war in Vietnam—though there is no record of him speaking out as he did on civil rights. He received his degree in the spring of 1967, making him eligible for the draft just as the war, in which more than a thousand Kentuckians lost their lives, entered its deadliest two-year stretch for American soldiers.

McConnell decided to enlist in the army reserves. With remarkable candor, he later said that the reserves represented a kind of "honorable alternative that wouldn't ruin my career or taint my advancement." Left unsaid was that the reserves also were much less likely to put him in harm's way, as they were used sparingly in Vietnam.

He reported for basic training with the 100th Division of the U.S. Army Reserves at Fort Knox in early July. Barely a month later, he was out, free on a medical discharge.

In McConnell's later telling, as related by Dyche, he discovered soon after he arrived at Fort Knox that he was having trouble keeping up with basic training, which he attributed to residual effects of the polio. A subsequent physical examination, he says, found that he suffered from optical neuritis, a condition most often associated with multiple sclerosis that can cause foggy vision or partial loss of vision. The condition can often be treated with steroids, but McConnell says the diagnosis of optical neuritis prompted the medical discharge. McConnell's Selective Service records, obtained from the National Archives under a public information request, do not specify the grounds for his discharge, and in fact show no record of his having received a physical examination prior to his discharge.

As short as his stay at Fort Knox had been, McConnell was growing impatient that his exit was taking as long as it was. By his own admission, he had his father place a call to his mentor in Washington. And on August 10, Senator John Sherman Cooper sent a wire to the commanding general at Fort Knox, stating: "Mitchell anxious to clear post in order to enroll NYU. Please advise when final action can be expected." Five days later, McConnell was discharged. Effective as Cooper's intervention had been, McConnell downplayed it years later, saying Cooper's office had been doing "routine case work" in trying to help a constituent deal with army bureaucracy. He had, he said, "used no connections getting in" the army reserves and "no connections getting out."

———————

Freed from Fort Knox, McConnell did not go to New York University, where there is no record of his ever having applied for classes, despite the claim in Cooper's missive. He'd had plenty of schooling, after all, and was ready for the business of politics. The only question was where to begin. Ideally, he'd have gone right back to Washington. But there wasn't all that much demand for a graduate of a non-elite law school with undistinguished grades. Even

Cooper was disinclined to help out in this regard, telling McConnell he had no need for a young counsel.

He'd have to settle for Kentucky, for now. He took the first legal job he could find—working for a pro-union labor law firm. But the drudgery of his first regular job would last barely longer than his military sojourn. In early 1968, Morton, the state's other senator, announced his retirement amid deep disillusionment over the urban riots and war in Vietnam. Marlow Cook, the moderate Republican executive for Jefferson County, which includes Louisville, announced his candidacy, and invited McConnell on as his campaign's "state youth chairman," a paid position. Mitch McConnell's near lifelong career as a political professional had begun.

He had some campaign experience. Back in 1966, in his campaign debut, he had helped out on a primary challenge of none other than his first Capitol Hill boss, Gene Snyder, by a liberal Louisville Republican—further confirmation of where McConnell had lined up in his party's internal conflicts. (Yet more evidence was the name he gave the cat he soon acquired: Rocky, after Nelson Rockefeller, the moderate Republican governor of New York.) But now he was a full-time campaign staffer for the first time, and he took the task earnestly, recalls John Yarmuth, then a younger campaign worker who was paired up with McConnell. It was quite a spectacle: there, in 1968, at the height of the youth rebellion, was the unimpeachably square law school graduate going from one campus to another, urging students fixated on Vietnam, Bob Dylan, and the assassinations of King and Bobby Kennedy to vote for a county executive many had never heard of. If he got a cool response, it did not deter him—he worked relentlessly, not even letting his marriage shortly before the primary to Sherrill Redmon, a history Ph.D. student at the University of Kentucky, slow him down. "He was incredibly serious even then," says Yarmuth, who went on to work alongside McConnell in Washington and Louisville and was later elected to Congress as a Democrat. "I was having fun or trying to have fun. Even though it was going to play a very small part of the election—organizing campuses in 1968 was a fragment of the whole election—to him it was very important."

The grind paid off—Cook won, and invited McConnell to Washington. Officially, McConnell was Cook's chief staffer on the Judiciary Committee. He helped his boss reckon with Richard Nixon's Supreme Court nominations, two of whom were rejected, one as too conservative and the other as underqualified. And he helped handle Cook's correspondence. In March 1970, he sent the Republican National Committee two speeches by Cook, which, McConnell wrote, "might be useful to you in your task of convincing both Blacks and other minority groups in the country that the Republican party is a logical home," a preoccupation of moderate Republicans at the time. Three months later, he declined the invitation of an honorary membership for himself and Cook in the Kentucky State Rifle & Pistol Association, writing that "this would probably hinder effectiveness in fighting [strict gun control] laws, if we were members of the association."

Unofficially, McConnell was a frontline foot-soldier in the era's intensifying battle for his party's soul. He lined up on the side of the moderates—his boss was a leading advocate for the Equal Rights Amendment, guaranteeing equal rights for women—but was wary of any talk among his increasingly despairing fellow moderates of breaking away from the GOP.

This debate even led McConnell to the pages of *Playboy*—not for the pictures, but for the articles. In 1970, the magazine published a manifesto by Lee Auspitz, president of the Ripon Society, the organization founded in 1962 to promote moderate Republicanism. McConnell fired off a letter to Auspitz praising the piece as the "most definitive explanation of liberal Republicanism I have read," while taking issue with the suggestion that had been made recently by some moderates that they ought to consider bolting the party. "The quickest way to completely eliminate our effectiveness within the GOP is to even suggest the possibility of withdrawing from our party," McConnell wrote. "The Nixon administration, to this point, has been at worst completely reactionary and at best totally indecisive. No one is more frustrated with this state of affairs than I. However, for all the reasons you stated in your *Playboy* article, this is the logical home for us and we must not give up."

He was a party man, above all, and the only question was when he'd make his official entrance under its banner. When the Nixon White House invited him to join the administration later in 1970, he fatefully declined, deciding it was time to head back to Kentucky and start his ascent from there. No sooner had he arrived home than he filed to run for a newly formed district in the Kentucky House of Representatives. He had moved to the district only two weeks before it became official, and his primary rivals challenged his candidacy under the Kentucky constitution, which requires candidates to reside in a given city or district for a year before running for office there. (McConnell, in an amusingly legalistic gambit, tried to argue that he could not have lived in the district for a year prior because the district hadn't existed yet.) It was an embarrassing debut for the candidate-in-waiting, already sensitive to his status as a nonnative of Kentucky. He was tossed off the ballot.

Launch aborted, the thirty-year-old McConnell pinged back and forth between home and Washington: he worked on an unsuccessful gubernatorial campaign in Kentucky, returned to Washington to help prepare William Rehnquist for his Supreme Court hearings, took an undemanding law job at the firm of a successful lawyer-turned-entrepreneur in Louisville just in time for the birth of his first child, then returned to Washington to serve as a deputy assistant attorney general in the Ford administration, deputized as a liaison to Congress on judicial appointments. On weekends, he'd fly home to Kentucky to see Sherrill and their baby.

Someone who didn't know any better might have taken McConnell as directionless, casting about while trying to care for his growing family (with three daughters, eventually). In fact, McConnell picked out his next target not long after his failed first run:

the county executive job in Jefferson County, which had propelled his former boss Marlow Cook into the U.S. Senate. It was an unusual position—technically called "County Judge/Executive," with some vestigial and nominal purview over the county courts—but essentially the elected chief administrator for the county, with particular purview for the fast-growing suburbs that extended beyond the Louisville city line, where the Louisville mayor's bailiwick stopped. It was the ideal position for an ambitious first-time candidate—unglamorous enough to be attainable, but with real responsibilities, in the state's largest jurisdiction, which held one in five Kentucky residents and many of the moderate to liberal Republicans, or even freethinking cosmopolitan Democrats, who fit McConnell's profile. He had positioned himself well by getting involved in the Jefferson County Republican Party, succeeding its deceased chairman in 1973.

Crucially, the incumbent was vulnerable. Todd Hollenbach was a handsome Notre Dame alumnus in a heavily Catholic city, but he'd come under fire for running a crony-laden, ethically challenged administration. The Binghams, the liberal-minded owners of the influential *Louisville Courier-Journal,* didn't care for him. (The feeling was mutual: "I didn't see eye to eye with young Barry Bingham," the publisher, Hollenbach says. "I told him respectfully that I didn't think there was anything wrong with this city that a handful of well-placed funerals wouldn't cure.") Hollenbach had also been having marital troubles before getting a divorce.

He'd won reelection by a huge margin in 1973. But shortly into his second term, he'd been caught up in the biggest storm to hit Louisville in decades—in 1974, a federal judge acting at the behest of the Sixth U.S. Circuit Court of Appeals issued a desegregation order for the Louisville schools, leading to the merger of the city and county districts, forced busing of 19,500 children, and protests from many white residents beyond the city line—Hollenbach's constituents. Hollenbach had tried to position himself as a reasoned critic of the rulings, saying he supported desegregation but preferred means other than busing to achieve it. He was, in any case, powerless to do much about them.

Into this opening stepped McConnell. The thirty-five-year-old had, to this point, done barely anything in Kentucky except some law firm drudgery and helping manage other people's campaigns. But he'd long been preparing for this moment, as suggested by his October 1975 letter offering President Gerald Ford his resignation from the Department of Justice job. After thanking Ford for the opportunity to serve, McConnell launched into a lament about the "discord" that busing had caused in Louisville, stated that he supported a constitutional amendment to prohibit it and, barring that, pleaded with Ford to nominate antibusing justices to the Supreme Court. It was a striking appeal from a junior staff member, particularly one who had a decade earlier joined the civil rights cause in Louisville.

But the motivation was plain to Bob Wolthus, a senior aide in the Ford administration, who wrote a memo to his supervisor that explained the context of McConnell's letter: "In 1977 Mitch plans to run for the post of county judge in the Louisville area as a Republican. He says the busing issue down there is a very big political factor and he would like to position himself to take advantage of it in the 1977 election."

As this plotting was under way, its target had no notion of what was coming his way. "I had never, quite frankly, heard of Mitch McConnell," says Hollenbach.

———

The young people on the campaign—that is, those even younger than the candidate himself—liked to practice a gentle sort of humor on him. McConnell slouched so much that Zane Griffin, his twenty-one-year-old scheduler, would pat him down and say, "What's all this stuff in your pockets?" "We'd give him posture lessons," she recalls. "We had fun with him—on his own terms."

It was hard to figure how someone who had spent so much

of his first dozen years out of college—or even longer than that—preparing for this moment could seem so ill-matched for it. To help loosen him up when he was out meeting voters, the campaign made sure he was always accompanied by his personal assistant, a handsome and affable young man by the name of Mike Baer, who radiated such confidence that a little of it couldn't help but pass into Mitch by osmosis. Aides with the candidate in public were charged with remembering names.

And it wasn't just in interacting with voters that McConnell's greenness shone. It was also in some of the basic backroom strategizing, recall Goodman and Plesser, his adman and pollster. "He was very ingenuous and very earnest—he did not have any of the sophistication or sensitivity to the political process and communications and the strategic management of elections," says Plesser. "Like a lot of newcomers, he'd think about it straightforwardly: let's speak to the issues. That's something that came to him a little later, the mechanics. For us, it was about giving him some orientation and insight into the ways that campaigns really worked."

Luckily, their candidate was open to that orientation. He assented to the consultants' suggestion that he break up the electorate into segments, by neighborhood and interest group, and create not just a message for each but, essentially, an image of himself for each. This strategy was not only a good way to relate to voters but was all but mandatory for someone like McConnell, who had such a nondescript profile. "Rather than being 'Mitch McConnell the lawyer,' and using that as a credential—that was meaningless—he became 'Mitch McConnell the county judge candidate who feels very strongly about the highway light,'" says Plesser.

One of the key segments McConnell set out to pursue was organized labor. For a Southern state, Kentucky had strong unions—unlike every state to its south, it is not "right to work"—and McConnell was running as such a moderate-to-liberal Republican that it was not inconceivable that he could get some labor support. Over and over, his scheduler, Griffin, tried to set up a meeting with one of the top leaders of the local AFL-CIO labor council. "I used my sweetest soft sell," she recalls. "I said, 'Can you meet him Monday? No? Tuesday? No? Wednesday? No? Thursday?' And he said, 'Thursday, that's my bowling day.' So I actually sent Mitch to bowling."

McConnell did not just go to the lanes. He told the unions that he would support passing a state law to legalize collective bargaining for public employees, a liberal position that even Hollenbach, the Democrat, had reservations about. It paid off: the labor council endorsed McConnell.

That McConnell was running to Hollenbach's left on some issues—he ran separate from the rest of the local Republican slate, and even got the endorsement of the *Courier-Journal*—complicated the question of how to go after Hollenbach over the busing issue. It was tempting to do so, given how much ill will it had stirred up in the county, and how well McConnell had set himself up as an opponent of busing with his letter to Ford. McConnell had the consultants make up a spot with him standing in front of a school bus saying, "Some say Judge Hollenbach could have done something about this. Some say he couldn't." But the campaign decided not to air it: the issue had already done its damage to Hollenbach.

Not that McConnell was going to play nice across the board. Goodman came up with a memorable spot, the defining one of the campaign, showing a farmer mucking out a horse's stall while commenting on Hollenbach's claim to have cut taxes four times. "When Hollenbach says he cut my taxes, he doesn't credit me with any more sense than old Nell here. Maybe Hollenbach ought to have my job, because in my business, I deal with that kind of stuff every day." The farmer closes by pitching a load of manure right at the camera. The ad, which debuted during the first game of the World Series, appalled some of McConnell's supporters in Louisville high society, but was a hit in less tony quarters. "Some of the nice people said, 'Ooh, that's pretty rough,'" says Goodman, the ad maker. "But the guys around the feed store said, 'Hey, that guy's got balls.'" One person who had no reservations about the ad was the candidate himself. "Oh, God, he loved it," says Goodman.

A couple of other ads turned the knife more subtly—the campaign went heavy on spots showing McConnell smiling happily with his wife and children, an obvious contrast with Hollenbach's splintering marriage, which also provided the subtext for an ad with a man in a clerical collar intoning, "Speaking for myself, I think that Mitch McConnell has the character that's been missing." (Hollenbach stews over this line of attack to this day. "It was just the *snideness* of his remarks, about how 'I feel so sorry for the children.' In my judgment, it was disgraceful and disgusting how he talked about it.") To cap it off, McConnell ran an ad showing himself strolling with his mentor John Sherman Cooper in Washington's Lafayette Park, with Cooper (who'd left the Senate in 1972) remarking, in an implicit rebuke to Hollenbach, that two terms was enough time for anyone to serve in office.

McConnell won by six percentage points. A giddy, raucous crowd assembled at the campaign office off Bardstown Road. It seemed like everyone who was anyone in Louisville had turned out for it. McConnell was beaming, and did something his staff had never seen him do before or in the years that followed. He told them he was taking them to lunch the following week at the Galt House, the city's new riverside hotel.

––––––

Mitch McConnell had made it into office, and seemed to have a good idea of what to do when he got there. He overhauled the upper levels of most departments and launched a methodical search for replacements that extended well beyond Louisville, a process that riled some old-timers in the county. (One of the Democratic county commissioners threw a punch at McConnell's closest aide, former college classmate Dave Huber.) He stocked his inner office with his top campaign aides—Huber, Runyon, and campaign manager

Joe Schiff—but also brought in Minx Auerbach, a leading Louis-ville liberal. He followed through on priorities he had laid out in the campaign, like the creation of an office of historic preservation and boosting spending on libraries.

One campaign pledge, though, was strikingly dropped: he never did push for collective bargaining for public employees. He later acknowledged, as related by John David Dyche, that his pledge was nothing more than "open pandering" to the unions.

Another of McConnell's most notable accomplishments as county leader was barely discernible to the public. With *Roe v. Wade* having legalized abortion in Kentucky only a few years prior, abortion opponents were trying to rein in the procedure via local ordinances that, among other restrictions, required married women to get their husbands' approval and imposed waiting periods. Abor-tion rights supporters had an ally in McConnell: every time one of the ordinances was introduced, McConnell would see to it that it never came up for a vote, much less a public hearing, says Jessica Loving, who was then the director of the Kentucky chapter of the American Civil Liberties Union. "He was one of the best elected officials I ever worked with in terms of dealing with the issue," she says. "He said, 'You're right, this flies in the face of *Roe v. Wade,*' and he just stopped the legislation dead in its tracks. . . . Mitch under-stood procedural ways to stop legislation, and that's what he did."

It was clear to her, she says, that McConnell was screening the ordinances not only on legal grounds but also because they clashed with his pro-choice leanings. "He had a very feminist perspective on it and I appreciated it," she said. Indeed, when Dolores Dela-hanty, another feminist activist in town, approached McConnell and asked if he would lend his name to a fund-raiser being held by the pro-choice Kentucky Women's Political Caucus, he assented. "He fully understood what the caucus was all about and where we stood on abortion," Delahanty says. "It was obvious to me that he supported the caucus in that regard." And Yarmuth recalls Mc-Connell as having been pro-choice when they worked together in

Cook's office. In turn, Schiff, McConnell's chief strategist, praised Yarmuth as a "good, progressive, pro-choice Republican" when he ran for the county board.

Loving kept McConnell's cooperation quiet at the time—one of the local ACLU's then-board members, Suzy Post, says she had no inkling of McConnell's assistance. And it wasn't hard to deduce why McConnell was happy to forgo public credit for these efforts. Just days into his county administration, Meme Runyon, now his press secretary, was given a list of all of Kentucky's newspapers and was instructed to start sending her news releases about Mc-Connell across the state. McConnell was already thinking how he would get to Washington—specifically, the Senate he so revered—which meant running for office beyond relatively liberal Jefferson County. "We were planning in those first three months a campaign that was going to take place eight years away," she says.

The problem was there was another election standing in the way, his county reelection in 1981. McConnell nearly lost it, to an uninspiring county commissioner. He'd lost his support from the unions after his betrayal on the collective-bargaining pledge; the recession of the early 1980s had voters in an anti-incumbent mood; and McConnell could no longer feature his family in ads, having divorced his wife, Sherrill Redmon, just a few years after so effectively deploying her against Hollenbach. (Dyche describes the end of the twelve-year marriage as "amicable" but "personally unpleasant." He also quotes Redmon hinting at the challenge of being married to a man whom she describes, euphemistically, as a "self-contained person.")

And McConnell by his own admission simply hadn't focused enough on the race. On election night, even as it became clear that he would survive, he was stewing over the numbers, wondering how he didn't get a bigger margin in this or that precinct. "Here's a guy winning reelection in this tough battle . . . and Tully and I are saying, this is real good, winning is better than losing," says Good-man. "But Mitch wasn't all that happy."

"He damn near got beat, which would've ended him—it would've ended his life," says Larry Forgy, a veteran Republican lawyer in Kentucky who served as Ronald Reagan's state campaign chairman in 1980, and later had a falling-out with McConnell. "I don't know what Mitch McConnell would do if not for politics."

McConnell had learned his lesson. He would never let his guard down, never take his eye off the next election.

And so he resumed the preparation that Runyon had started for him in 1978 with those statewide press releases on the doings of the Jefferson County judge/executive. Even better than sending press releases to every county paper, he realized, was having a reason to visit every corner of the state himself. And partway through his second term, he found a reason: his aide Bill Bardenwerper returned from a visit to the Chicago police department, where he'd learned about an underage prostitution ring that had tentacles to Louisville. McConnell jumped on the issue—he called for expanded fingerprinting of children, held hearings across the state, and created a "Statewide Task Force on Exploited and Missing Children," which produced state legislation, passed into law by the Democratic-led legislature, that included preventive measures and stiffer penalties for child trafficking.

Bardenwerper insists that the motivation was not entirely political. "Cynics criticized Mitch for making politics out of the issue, but I always said he could have been on the wrong side of the issue, like some members of Congress turned out to be in their various sordid personal lives," he says. "If you get a politician on the right side of right, no matter the motivation, how can that be bad?" Still, he and others acknowledge the dividends that the crusade paid. It helped get McConnell to every one of the state's 120 counties in 1983 and 1984, and gave him an identity that went beyond a lawyer turned county administrator from Louisville. "The child abuse thing went around the state," says one former Republican officeholder in the state, "so it was, rather than 'oh, that's the lawyer guy,' 'oh, that's the child abuse guy.'"

Preparation came in another form, too. Frustrated with how close he'd come to losing his reelection, McConnell decided it was time for a new media and polling team. Goodman and Plesser, who had delivered McConnell his big win against Hollenbach, were out. Now McConnell wanted nothing less than the best. In 1984, he hired Roger Ailes.

Ailes was still a dozen years from founding Fox News, but his reputation was already well established. After meeting Richard Nixon backstage at *The Mike Douglas Show,* which he helped produce, he'd been brought on to tutor the dour candidate in the ways of television for the 1968 campaign. After stormy forays into theater and TV news, he was by the early 1980s specializing in creating ads for Republican Senate candidates. There was no mystery what you were getting when you hired Ailes as your adman—hard-hitting spots that went straight for the opponent's weak spot. Factual accuracy was not a priority. To elect Alphonse D'Amato senator in New York, that meant highlighting his opponent Liz Holtzman's unmarried status. To reelect Harrison "Jack" Schmitt in New Mexico, that meant producing an ad that accused his opponent, state attorney general Jeff Bingaman, of having freed a "convicted felon" on the FBI's Most Wanted List. As Gabriel Sherman notes in his biography of Ailes, the FBI had "requested [the convict's] temporary release into its custody in order for him to testify as a key prosecution witness at a trial in Texas for the murder of a judge." Asked about the ad, Ailes said it was Bingaman's job to point out the context of the felon's release. "My responsibility ends with the act. Maybe folks can say I'm an unethical guy. But it's not my job to make . . . Bingaman's case."

Ailes brought with him not only an unrestrained approach to the business of making ads but a penchant for personal drama. He was known to get into physical scuffles with coworkers and once punched a hole through the wall of the control room of the NBC late-night talk show where he worked. His personal style could hardly have been in starker contrast to that of the buttoned-down

McConnell, for whom cutting loose meant sitting back with his aides in the county office after work to sip from the bottle of Old Forester bourbon he kept on hand.

But Ailes and McConnell shared one thing in common. And it trumped all difference, as well as any misgivings McConnell might have about hiring someone with an unscrupulous reputation. As Janet Mullins, McConnell's manager for the coming campaign, later recalled: "Roger lived it and breathed it and wanted to win as badly as Mitch did." Or as Ailes himself put it in his favorite office mantra: "Whatever it takes."

The person unfortunate enough to find himself in the sights of McConnell's new hire was a second-term senator named Walter "Dee" Huddleston, a World War II tank gunner who'd entered politics after several decades in the radio business. He had won the race to succeed the retiring John Sherman Cooper. Now Cooper's protégé wanted the seat back.

Huddleston was well liked and politically in tune with his constituents, a quintessential Southern Democrat. But like Todd Hollenbach, he did not realize what he was up against with this mild-mannered young Louisville lawyer. This miscalculation was understandable, to a degree—if Mitch McConnell had seemed ill-suited to campaigning among his fellow Louisvillians, he seemed even more so out in the state's outlying areas. He did his best to develop what Joe Whittle, the Republican state chairman at the time, calls his "mountain presentation," but he was never going to be as natural with rural voters as, say, Gene Snyder, who, on visiting country stores, was known to pull out a knife and start whittling some wood.

McConnell, on the other hand, "hasn't enough personality to wash a shotgun," as Forgy, who in 1984 was again serving as Reagan's campaign chairman, puts it. It didn't help McConnell in the common-touch department that he was often carrying around a briefcase, an accessory that Forgy suspected was totally for show—a ploy by Ailes to make the youthful-looking forty-two-year-old look more senatorial. "I remember once, in Bowling Green, [Vice President George H. W.] Bush came to speak and said, 'What's he doing? Why does he have that briefcase with him?'" Forgy recalls. But regardless of the quips, McConnell persisted. "Most people wouldn't be willing to carry around a briefcase that's empty," says Forgy. "You'd say, 'Shit, I'm not going to do that.' But he did it. . . . Whatever they were telling him to do, he did."

No Republican had won a statewide election in the state since Cooper's big win in 1966. To plot a path to victory, McConnell's new pollster, Lance Tarrance from Houston—whom McConnell had courted with two separate trips to the Kentucky Derby—had segmented the electorate into five different groups: registered Republicans, younger suburban ticket-splitters, white conservative Democrats, white liberal Democrats, and black voters, who tilted Democratic. Even if McConnell got nearly all of the first group and the vast majority of the second, that still left him only at about 40 percent. The "key to everything," Tarrance says, was the white conservative Democrats. If he could get more than a third of them, then he might pull it off.

Except McConnell's numbers with these conservative Democrats were, if anything, declining over the summer of 1984 in the surveys Tarrance was doing. "We were sixty days out, and I told him, if this continues, we're not going to get it," Tarrance says. As Ailes recalled: "He was so far behind we almost had to flip a coin about who was going to give him the bad news."

————

One Saturday night, Tarrance received an excited call from Ailes. "He told me he'd just finished with some wild and crazy ads that might blow up the campaign or might save it," Tarrance says. Ailes sent the scripts to Tarrance by express mail. "They were brilliant," says Tarrance. "Even though they were right out of *Hee Haw*."

As Ailes later told it, he'd been watching TV at home that weekend when an ad for dog food came on, with a pack of dogs scurrying after a bag of kibble. This ad had stirred a recollection of a tidbit a campaign researcher had noted, that Huddleston had missed several important votes while giving paid speeches around the country (which senators were then allowed to do). Sherman, in his Ailes biography, describes the rest of the creative epiphany:

> *Ailes jotted down the word "Dogs!" on a piece of paper. During a strategy meeting, Ailes presented his vision. McConnell's campaign manager, Janet Mullins, recalled the moment: "There was Roger, sitting in a cloud of pipe smoke, and he said, 'This is Kentucky. I see hunting dogs. I see hound dogs on the scent looking for the lost member of Congress.'"*

Thus was born a classic of the attack ad genre. Larry McCarthy, the Ailes associate who would go on to fame for crafting the Willie Horton ad against Michael Dukakis in the 1988 presidential campaign, was put in charge of finding dogs and a trainer. This task proved difficult—McCarthy first came back with bluetick hounds, which were deemed not true Kentucky hounds. He went out for different ones. "If you're going to be culturally calling someone on the carpet, you better have your cultural facts right," says Tarrance. "We threw everything we had at this, because we had maxed out everything else we could do." Finally, it was ready: A pack of bloodhounds straining on their leashes head off from Capitol Hill, through the woods, across a beach, past a swimming pool, with this voice-over, scripted by Ailes: "My job was to find Dee Huddleston and get him back to work. Huddleston was skipping votes but making an extra fifty thousand dollars giving speeches. Let's go, boys!"

The charge that Huddleston was playing widespread hooky was, as *Newsweek* noted at the time, "baseless": Huddleston was present for 94 percent of votes. McConnell himself later admitted that an accompanying radio ad attacking Huddleston for his attendance at committee meetings was "fundamentally unfair" and "kind of ridiculous." But the line of attack rang true, given that the phlegmatic Huddleston was running such a lackluster campaign. Voters ate it up—especially the conservative Democrats who might otherwise be left cool by the Louisville lawyer with the briefcase. "People would say, 'Mitch, what about the coon hounds!'" says Whittle, who was often with McConnell on the trail. And McConnell's numbers with that key segment surged.

Still, McConnell had not yet closed the gap, and an air of desperation was settling over the campaign. Never had Tarrance seen a candidate as on edge as McConnell in those final weeks. "He was pretty psychologically uptight, that's as nice as I can put it," Tarrance says. "He knew this was his one chance to make a breakout. It was all on the line. He kept using the phrase 'We need to find the silver bullet,' something to put us over fifty percent. . . . I've never been on a campaign before or since with so much physical tension to find the key that would finally open the door." He adds, "Everything you discussed with Mitch was how to climb the mountain. There was no laughing, no joking." Tarrance and Ailes had no shortage of campaigns to advise that year, he said, but on none of them were they working nearly as hard as for Mitch McConnell.

The campaign decided their best bet was to go back to the dogs one more time, at the risk of overdoing it. They aired a sequel in which the hound dogs find Huddleston, played by a look-alike actor, cowering way up in a tree.

That might have done it. McConnell won, just barely, by a margin of five thousand votes—four-tenths of a percentage point, about one vote per precinct. At the Republican victory party in Louisville, Gene Snyder, McConnell's first boss in Washington, was overheard remarking with wry wonderment that Kentuckians had just elected to the U.S. Senate someone who had fewer friends in Kentucky than "anybody elected to anything."

———

McConnell's margin of victory was particularly narrow in contrast to the more than 283,000 votes by which another Republican won that night in Kentucky: Ronald Reagan.

McConnell had an ambivalent relationship with the president. He was, after all, no Ronald Reagan Republican—in keeping with his John Sherman Cooper inheritance, he had backed Gerald Ford in 1976 and George H. W. Bush in 1980 over the conservative ex-governor from California (not only that, he had privately ranked Reagan *fourth* among Republican candidates in 1980). But with Reagan near the peak of his popularity in 1984 and running against Walter Mondale, a liberal Minnesotan with little appeal for Kentucky swing voters—especially those conservative Democrats who were the key to his election—McConnell had done his utmost to associate himself with the top of the ticket. Whittle, the state party chairman, had made it a refrain to tell voters around the state that Reagan "needs Mitch" in Washington. McConnell's team, lacking campaign chairmen in many of the state's counties, had asked the Reagan campaign if its county chairmen could double in that role for McConnell.

While the Reagan campaign agreed to that request, the eagerness for association had not been mutual. When Reagan came to Louisville for one of his debates against Mondale, a visit McConnell's campaign hyped as much as it could, the president referred to the candidate as "O'Donnell." But that slight had done nothing to diminish the tug of Reagan's coattails. It was a political scientist's axiom: if the top of the ticket is pulling 60 percent or more of the vote, there is a coattail effect for candidates farther down the ticket. "It helped a lot," says Whittle. "Anytime you have someone like Ronald Reagan anyplace that's conservative, it's going to help the party down the line, down to sheriff. I hate to say that's the whole thing, but in order to win Kentucky, you've got to get the Republicans out," and Reagan did that for McConnell. Hollenbach,

McConnell's 1977 opponent, is blunter: "If you take away . . . Ronald Reagan, there is no Mitch McConnell."

It was because Reagan's impact on McConnell's election was so obvious that people attending the GOP election night party in Louisville were so startled when McConnell, in his victory speech, did not acknowledge the president at all. After seeking to bask in Reagan's reflected glow throughout the campaign, McConnell did not want to share the spotlight. "He never mentioned Reagan. He never said, 'I appreciate the margin Reagan provided,'" says Forgy, Reagan's Kentucky campaign chairman. When reporters asked Forgy that night about McConnell's victory, he was candid. "I said, 'Hell, Reagan's coattails were as long as a bedsheet.'" When quotes to this effect appeared in the press the next morning, Forgy heard from McConnell. "He called me the next day and said, 'Don't say that anymore,'" Forgy says. "He didn't want the Democrats to pick up on the fact that he was a political fluke—that he didn't get there by an intentional process."

McConnell was at a loss about how to discuss his victory. When Tully Plesser, his former pollster, called him after the election to congratulate him, McConnell told him that the press was "hounding him" about what he thought was key to his victory, and said that he had credited Ailes's ad, rather than Reagan. Plesser told McConnell that this answer was wrong. "I told him to say that you won because your positions coincided with the interests of the voters. Not because a very skilled and manipulative operative pulled a stunt on your behalf."

McConnell took this advice. From that point on, his account of his election to the Senate left out both Reagan and Ailes. This omission did not endear him with Ailes, or with others who had worked so hard on that high-pressure campaign. "McConnell read too much into himself instead of Ailes in the first case and Reagan in the second," says Tarrance. The lack of gratitude became more glaring a few years later when McConnell put out word that he was going to make his 1984 team reapply for the job for his reelection, just as he had decided to shop around for new advisers after his county campaigns.

Tarrance found this obnoxious in the extreme. "We suddenly saw a different McConnell," he said. "He was arrogant and disloyal to the people that put him there." Tarrance flew up from Houston to meet with McConnell but found him "cold and arrogant and not very loyal to his team. He really pissed me off." Tarrance told McConnell that he wasn't going to take the job even if offered, and left. A McConnell aide called him at the airport to get him to change his mind, to no avail. Ailes grudgingly decided to stay on and do some ads for McConnell, though in a reduced capacity. "Ailes and I had put together a pretty good team, and it was like McConnell was breaking his team," says Tarrance. "I'll fight to the death, but not for someone I don't believe in. Roger . . . said, 'I'll go and do it,' but we both lost a lot of respect for him."

The irony was, even as McConnell was seeking to downplay Reagan's role in his election, he was working to align himself with the conservative president. Leading up to and during his campaign, the Ripon Society's political arm, the New Leadership Fund, had touted McConnell as a moderate Republican on the rise. But on arriving in Washington, he confounded such expectations. He supported Reagan's plan to arm the Contras against Nicaragua's Sandinista government. He won conservative plaudits for pushing tort reform proposals (he came up with a "Sue for a Million Award" gimmick to highlight egregious tort claims). He broke with the agreement Huddleston and his fellow Democratic senator Wendell Ford had crafted for picking federal judges in Kentucky, a judicial nominating commission that McConnell decided was undermining his and Reagan's prerogative to select conservative judges.

And, to the dismay of Jessica Loving and his other abortion rights allies in Louisville, McConnell flipped to the pro-life side on votes such as blocking Medicaid funding for abortions in cases of rape or incest. (Years later, Loving ran into McConnell at a cocktail party at the University of Louisville and told him, "By the way, I've never properly thanked you for what you did—you were the best elected official for the pro-choice issue," to which, she recalls, "he got this pained look, his face got paler than usual and his lips got thinner than usual and he said, 'You know, I don't really want anyone to know that.'")

Most strikingly, perhaps, McConnell took up the fight for his party against legislation that was championed by his fellow Kentucky senator, Wendell Ford, calling for expanding voter participation by allowing citizens to register to vote when getting their driver's license. McConnell was candid about his reasons for opposing the "Motor Voter" bill—expanded voter registration helped Democrats, he said. He went so far as to suggest that low voter turnout was preferable in general: it is "a sign of the health of our democracy that people feel secure enough about the health of the country and about its leaders where they don't have to obsess about politics all the time." (A decade later, he would take the lead in pushing for voter identification requirements in the big 2002 election reform bill, thereby opening a major new front in his party's push to limit access to the polls.)

McConnell had warned of a coming rightward tack as he prepared to run for Senate, telling Keith Runyon, a *Courier-Journal* editorial writer and husband of McConnell's former aide Meme Sweets Runyon, that running for statewide office would require some adaptive coloration. "He told me he was going to change, because his electorate would change," Runyon says. But in later explaining to Kleber, the historian, and Dyche, the authorized biographer, the sheer extent of his rightward shift on arriving in Washington, McConnell pointed to a different explanation. Even if he had not been a Ronald Reagan man, he had watched Reagan win, and win big. The Senate Republican caucus he was arriving in was notably more conservative than it had been in the previous session. "The Capitol Hill rookie did not need a political compass to notice that the GOP had enjoyed considerable electoral success as it had moved rightward. Having gone with that flow, he now found himself in Washington," writes Dyche, paraphrasing McConnell. "Ronald Reagan . . . provided a powerful example that conservatism could work both in practice and politically" and McConnell "saw [conservatism's] adherents endure both bad polls and bad press and still win."

For someone who had almost lost, and didn't want to come that close to losing again, the moral of the story was clear.

———

Back in 1981, after his reelection as Jefferson County executive, McConnell had called up Harvey Sloane, the Democrat just elected to his second term as mayor of Louisville, and suggested they meet for breakfast. Sloane invited him to his house. There, the two agreed that it would be in the interest of both to work together as much as possible, given their overlapping jurisdictions and their shared ambitions for higher office. "We talked about the fact that we both had other aspirations, that the worst thing to do was to have two chief executives bickering," Sloane recalls. "It was: 'We're going to run for future office, so let's not cut each other up.'" The agreement held. The two men worked together on the delicate task of pushing for a merger of the city and county governments, which failed twice despite their effort.

There was no expectation the truce would outlive their time in adjacent office, and it did not. In 1989, Sloane announced he would challenge McConnell for the Senate the next year. He was a formidable candidate with a singular profile: the Yale-educated scion of a wealthy Northeastern family who had sloughed off his privilege to serve as a surgeon in eastern Kentucky and later in South Vietnam before setting up a clinic in Louisville's mostly African-American west end. After his two terms as mayor, he'd gone on to serve in McConnell's old seat as county executive. His fair and slender good looks recalled actor Alan Alda or former New York mayor John Lindsay.

McConnell wasted no time in turning that distinctive profile against Sloane. At Fancy Farm, the traditional political picnic in far western Kentucky that kicks off every election season, McConnell ripped into his former Jefferson County counterpart, the man who'd invited him over to his house, as the "wimp from the East" whose "mommy left him a million dollars" and who had "come down here to save us from ourselves." He mocked Sloane's vacation home in a "foreign country." (Unmentioned: it was in the sunny paradise of Canada.)

Meanwhile, back in Washington, McConnell set about establishing a voting record that would position him well against the dashing doctor, even if it meant going against his better instincts on public policy. He introduced an amendment to the defense spending bill to allow police to shoot down planes they suspected of carrying drugs (it was, he later admitted, one of the "most ridiculous" legislative gambits he'd ever engaged in). He voted for family leave legislation opposed by President Bush to deny Sloane the issue on the trail (just "chickened out," he later said). He introduced legislation for a $21 billion, five-year health-care program that went nowhere on the Hill but gave him something to counter Sloane's top issue, a call for national health insurance. "He had never done anything before or since to help people get health insurance," says Sloane, looking back.

By the summer of 1990, McConnell had outraised Sloane by a 3–1 margin, but was unable to open up a comfortable lead in the polls. His team resorted to a classic dirty trick: a McConnell campaign staffer called in to a TV show that Sloane was appearing on and, pretending to be an adulatory liberal, thanked him for making Louisville a "nuclear-free zone." This call spurred Sloane into a critique of nuclear power. In no time, the McConnell team had a tape of Sloane's comments circulating in western Kentucky, where the biggest employer was the Paducah nuclear enrichment plant.

Still, Sloane was making it competitive—a late October poll showed him slicing McConnell's lead in half, to 10 points. But

McConnell had one more card to play. Late that month, his campaign leaked to the press that Sloane had renewed a prescription for his sleeping pills using his expired Drug Enforcement Administration registration number (he'd stopped practicing some years earlier). Sloane said he needed the pills to deal with severe pain in his hip and back (he had hip replacement surgery after the election). The state's medical licensure board chided Sloane for the self-prescription but said no formal sanction was warranted. This did not stop McConnell, who, with Ailes still overseeing his television ads, put out brutal spots with images of vials and pills and a narrator forebodingly describing Sloane's penchant for prescribing "mood-altering," "powerful depressants" for himself at "double the safe dose without a legal permit."

Nearly a quarter century later, Sloane recalls the mortification of having a reporter approach him on the street the day of the leak and asking him about the prescription. But in a way, he knew it was coming. "Nothing surprised me about Mitch. That's the way he acts and campaigns and any mole he can uncover, he's going to do it. It's as negative as you can get," he says. "He's a guy without a lot of qualms in terms of how he conducts himself in campaigns." Frank Greer, Sloane's campaign manager, still seethes over the prescription attack. "This was something private that shouldn't have been public, that was distorted, that had to do with family issues." When Jim Cauley, a Democratic operative from Kentucky working on the campaign, saw McConnell's ad with the pills, he knew the race was over. "Oh my God, I just thought we were toast," he says. "Harvey is a good, honest human. That they did that to him pissed me off more than it surprised me. You take a guy who moves to Kentucky and opens up a health center in West Louisville—how do you make that bad? Well, they did. They take good people and make them bad."

On Election Day, McConnell edged Sloane by under 5 percentage points. It would be the narrowest of all his reelections, and one he was particularly proud of, relays Dyche: McConnell "considered his campaign as the best run in America that year." After all, he had won.

———

The pattern had been set. Every six years, McConnell would deploy pretty much the same strategy against whichever Democrat emerged to challenge him.

He would cast votes in Washington with the election foremost in mind. In 1996, running against former state attorney general and lieutenant governor Steve Beshear, he voted for an increase in the minimum wage even though it came without the business tax relief he thought any wage increase should be paired with. In 2008, he voted to override President George W. Bush's veto of a massive farm bill—he had managed to slip a special tax provision for racehorse owners into the bill, and breaking with the deeply unpopular president would help McConnell's reelection odds.

He would build up so massive a campaign account that it would scare off credible potential challengers who lacked the personal wealth or tolerance for the fund-raising that would be necessary to compete. In 2008, a difficult year for Republicans, McConnell came into January having already raised nearly $11 million, a whopping sum for so early in the season. The best the Democrats could come up with to take that on was Bruce Lunsford, who had lost two gubernatorial primaries but had the advantage of a personal fortune made in the nursing home business. Even that only went so far—by the final weeks of the race, when Lunsford was closing in the polls following the worldwide financial collapse, McConnell had nearly $6 million of the $18 million he had raised still on hand. Lunsford had raised only a third as much and had less than a quarter as much left to use.

And with this money at his disposal, McConnell would set about countering voters' lukewarm feelings toward him by doing what had worked so well against Sloane: He would make his opponents unacceptable. And he would make them unacceptable in the same way: he would cast them, as he had done Sloane, as elitists out of touch with working-class Kentuckians, even if it meant attacking wealth and success in business in ways that might make many Republicans uncomfortable. He mocked Beshear for his fondness for foxhunting: "Can you imagine a working-class hero who wears a hunting pink and brandishes a riding crop?" He ran an ad attacking his 2002 challenger, Lois Combs Weinberg, the daughter of a former Kentucky governor, for owning a house in the Virgin Islands. He hit Lunsford for owning homes in multiple states and for questions about his health-care companies.

It was a remarkable strategy, year in and year out, given that McConnell was not exactly tilling the bluegrass himself. He was as citified as they come. His Kentucky home was a townhouse in Louisville a few blocks from a trendy commercial district with coffeehouses and shops that now carry "Louisville: The Gayest City in Kentucky" T-shirts. (In Washington, he lived in a Capitol Hill townhouse where neighbors saw him come out on a regular basis with a broom in hand to sweep away every last bit of leaf or twig from his stoop.) Early in his career, he had tooled around Louisville in a little sports car. And he was, by his 1996 race, a wealthy man from his marriage in 1993 to Elaine Chao, the daughter of a Taiwanese shipping magnate.

Yet the populist attacks kept coming, to the astonishment of his opponents. "He did all that shit about [Beshear] foxhunting, about him being an elitist—Steve had two or three million dollars to McConnell's nine!" says Jim Cauley, who'd gone on to manage Beshear's campaign. Lunsford shrugged about the attack on his wealth and business, even if McConnell was, by 2008, himself worth as much as $13 million. "In a state as poor as Kentucky, that's an easy target," Lunsford said. "Why wouldn't you do that?" Lunsford said he never thought of countering by pointing out McConnell's own fortune, because he knew that much of it had come from Chao.

Chao's wealth was not only hard to use against McConnell, but his campaign was adept at deploying Chao, with her cheery demeanor, to humanize her dour husband. Lunsford couldn't help but wonder if Chao was so present on the campaign trail in 2008 to highlight that he himself was single. "My initial reaction was to say, 'He brought in the secretary of labor [Chao's government position at that point] to keep his job.'" But he decided that "that was hard to do when a woman is as nice as she is. If she was considered a bitch, it would've been different."

————

McConnell's approach of rendering the opposition unacceptable could be discerned in other political races, as well. In 1997, in his third try, he was named head of the National Republican Senatorial Committee—the campaign organ for GOP senators—thus extending his hand into races across the country. And he was also becoming active in races back home, taking it upon himself to speed the state's shift into the Republican column (a 1994 victory he engineered in a special election for an open congressional seat in a Democratic-leaning Kentucky district was a harbinger for the GOP sweep that fall). In 1998, he encouraged state legislator Ernie Fletcher to run for Congress against a Democrat who, as a public defender, had represented a man charged with raping and shooting a woman. The victim appeared in a Fletcher ad attacking his opponent for taking the case. The Kentucky Bar Association and *Lexington Herald-Leader* editorialists protested, but the ad swung the polls toward Fletcher, and McConnell later said, as related by Dyche, that he found it "legitimate" to attack a lawyer in that way. "I mean, I think you make a conscious decision in picking your clientele," he said.

That same year, the NRSC, under McConnell's leadership, provided funding for an ad before Election Day attacking the Democratic congressman Scotty Baesler, who was running against Jim Bunning, the former major league pitcher, for Kentucky's other Senate seat. The ad cited Baesler's vote for the North American Free Trade Agreement—with a swarthy Mexican actor saying,

"Muchas gracias, Señor Baesler." This scene was followed by the line, "But he also voted to give China special trade privileges, even though they're shuttin' out Kentucky-made products," accompanied with Chinese music and, in Cantonese: "Thank you, Scotty Baesler."

Six years later, Bunning was flailing in his race against Daniel Mongiardo, a state senator and physician from eastern Kentucky. On a bus caravan around the state with Bunning eight days before Election Day, Republican state senate president David Williams, a longtime McConnell ally, called Mongiardo, who was unmarried, "limp-wristed" and a "switch hitter." Another Republican senator, Elizabeth Tori, said she questioned whether "the word 'man' applies to" Mongiardo. Tori later said that if listeners took this to refer to Mongiardo's sexuality, "so be it."

By his own admission in later accounts, McConnell advised Bunning against rebuffing these comments. McConnell urged a redoubling of attacks on Mongiardo in the final days of the campaign on the issue that had emerged as a rallying cry for Republicans in that year's presidential election: same-sex marriage. The issue was also boiling at the state level, with a question on the Kentucky ballot to amend the state constitution to ban gay marriage. That Mongiardo himself supported that amendment did not stop McConnell. He conceived of an ad that linked Mongiardo and John Kerry in their opposition to a *national* constitutional amendment defining marriage as between a man and a woman.

Looking back, Mongiardo has no doubt that the Williams and Tori comments and same-sex marriage ads were an organized effort to "make people in Kentucky believe I was gay because I was single at the time . . . they were almost directly saying, this guy is gay—don't vote for him." And he has no doubt who was behind it. "Anything that happened in the Republican Party in the last twenty-five years in Kentucky, Mitch McConnell has been the orchestrator of. He has been the puppet master. Nothing happens in this state without his direct knowledge, his control. And while he's good at keeping his hands off things, no question his fingerprints were all over it."

The whole spectacle flabbergasted Mongiardo. He had closed to a tie in the polls with the increasingly erratic Bunning, who had at one point declared that Mongiardo resembled Saddam Hussein's sons and at another point confessed to no longer following the news. Then came Williams's and Tori's comments, and there was Mongiardo, campaigning in front of a large crowd at a shopping center, when a TV reporter marched right up to him and asked him point-blank if he was gay. "I answered it truthfully, honestly. I just said, 'No.'" What astonished him was how blatant it was. "They were desperate—they saw the direction the campaign was going in. They couldn't take a chance on doing it quietly. And obviously they were right—it worked as far as politics goes, so, you've got to hand it to them."

Mongiardo still runs his practice in Hazard. He is now married, and he and his wife have two children.

———

By the first decade of the twenty-first century, Mitch McConnell was claiming some big Kentucky marks. In 2002, he had broken John Sherman Cooper's record for the biggest margin of victory in a Senate election in Kentucky, in a race that he declared he had run "stronger than mule piss," better even than the "first-class ass-kicking" he had delivered to Beshear in 1996. In 2009, he had surpassed Wendell Ford's tenure as the longest-serving senator in the state's history. His work on behalf of other Kentucky Republicans, particularly in formerly Democratic western Kentucky, had put all but one of the state's six congressional districts in Republican hands. (However, Kentucky lagged behind the Republican ascendance in the rest of the South, with its House of Representatives still in Democratic control and only a single Republican governor since 1971.)

It was an unlikely record of electoral success, says Don Vish, a Louisville lawyer who first met McConnell when they worked

together on the 1966 primary campaign against Gene Snyder.
"You would never think he was headed in the direction he ended
up," Vish says. "You think of political people with great charisma
and smiles and pals and everybody's a friend and hail-fellow-well-
met—well, this is quite unfriendly territory for him. It's like finding
a plant that is growing in soil that shouldn't really be able to support the plant. Mitch is fairly urbane and looks and talks like he is
from the city, and Kentucky has always regarded Louisville like a
foreign country. He's always had so many strikes against him—he's
like a column of numbers that don't add up—you always get more
in the bottom than there was at the top."

To what end? McConnell's mentor Cooper had left his mark
in any number of areas—standing up to Joe McCarthy; resisting
a push to remove the Fifth Amendment's protection for reluctant
witnesses against self-incrimination; restraining U.S. military in-
volvement in Cambodia, Laos, and Thailand during the Vietnam
War. Another legendary Kentucky senator, Democratic majority leader Alben Barkley, had helped power New Deal legislation
through Congress before resigning his leadership post in protest
in a dispute with Franklin D. Roosevelt over tax legislation. Long
before that, of course, Henry Clay had brokered the great com-
promises that sought to resolve the growing nation's burgeoning
conflict over slavery.

McConnell had developed his own area of expertise, an issue
he cared about deeply. It was not always the most popular thing
to be seen fighting for, which might have seemed at odds with
his perennial fixation on setting himself up for victory in the next
election cycle. But at its essence, the issue was utterly consistent
with that goal.

Chapter Two

NO MONEY DOWN

The collapse came in the middle of the night, on October 11, 2000. Three hundred million gallons of coal slurry, the viscous mix of mud, coal waste, and chemicals left as a by-product from purifying coal, broke through the inadequate buffer that separated the sixty-eight-acre holding pond of the Martin County Coal Corporation's Big Branch Refuse Impoundment from the surrounding mine. The dark sludge poured through two miles of mine tunnels—a miner had left the area just moments earlier—before oozing out of a mountainside opening into the hilly landscape of far eastern Kentucky. It found its way into two tributaries of the Big Sandy River—first Coldwater Creek, and then, after the pressure forced a break in the other side of the impoundment, into Wolf Creek—filling them ever higher until it overran embankments, spreading toward the homes lining the creek bottoms of Inez, the 500-person town that Lyndon Baines Johnson visited in 1964 to promote his War on Poverty, and covering their yards with a vast moat of goop that rose to six feet deep in places. Inez resident Mickey McCoy threw golf-ball-size rocks into the blackened creeks and watched as they refused to sink in the noxious pudding. "It was a slow-moving black smothering," he says. There was no immediate effort by the company to alert the townspeople sleeping in the spill's path—Abraham Lincoln "Linc" Chapman didn't know about the sludge until he encountered it while heading up Coldwater Creek before daybreak to bow-hunt deer. "It was a lot of chaos," he says. "If you never saw a slurry spill it's hard to describe it. It was like a lava flow coming down the creek bed." His nine-year-old daughter was so terrorized by the advancing slop that he would later build another story onto their house, as a refuge from future assaults.

In the sheer scale of contamination, it was a much larger disaster than even the 1989 spill of 11 million gallons of crude oil into Alaska's Prince William Sound by the *Exxon Valdez*. As documented in reports by *Washington Monthly* and *Salon* and a documentary film by Robert Salyer, the slurry's seventy-five-mile course of destruction downstream to the Ohio River killed 1.6 million fish and countless wildlife that got stuck in the muck or drank from it; carried away roads and bridges; and contaminated the water systems of more than 27,000 people (a 2001 study by the Environmental Protection Agency found up to thirty times the typical levels of arsenic and mercury in Inez's groundwater). The cleanup only exacerbated the damage, as trucks and other heavy equipment rolled onto people's lawns, ripping up gas lines and knocking over trees. Later "creek bank reconstruction" efforts resulted in widespread tree removal and in many places only exacerbated erosion. "People's property just gets eaten off and falls," says Chapman. The only consolation was the miraculous lack of any loss of human life (though many residents reported suffering from rashes and respiratory problems). A 1972 slurry flood following a dam break in Buffalo Creek, across the border in Logan County, West Virginia, had claimed the lives of 125 people; had the Martin Creek spill surged entirely into Coldwater Creek instead of being diverted into Wolf Creek as well, it could have swept away hundreds of townspeople.

The U.S. Department of Labor's Mine Safety and Health Administration kicked into gear, with an investigative team led by Tony Oppegard, a senior political appointee. His second in command was Jack Spadaro, a career MSHA engineer. As a twenty-three-year-old new hire at the agency, Spadaro had worked on the

Buffalo Creek investigation and was haunted by it still. The team found a trail of clues implicating both Martin County Coal's owner, the mining giant Massey Energy, and their own agency, most notably a 1994 recommendation by an MSHA engineer, following a slurry spill at the same impoundment earlier that year, that Martin County Coal needed to carry out a host of recommendations before it could resume using the holding pond. Martin County Coal had failed to carry out the recommendations, and MSHA had failed to follow up on them. The rock and earthen wall separating the pond and the adjacent mine was as thin as 15 feet in spots—far below the 150 feet recommended by MSHA, far below the 70 feet Martin County Coal had claimed it to be on a map submitted to MSHA, and far too meager to hold back the pond, which was 80 feet deep at the time of the break. Oppegard and Spadaro's team of investigators was on its way to preparing to bring eight separate violations against Massey that together could have resulted in hundreds of thousands of dollars of fines and laid the foundation for charges of willful and criminal negligence. "It's a crazy thing to build an impoundment over an active coal mine," says Oppegard.

As their investigation in deepest Appalachia proceeded, though, another process had been dragging out in sunny Florida. And on December 12, with a 5–4 ruling by the Supreme Court reversing the Florida Supreme Court's call for a statewide recount of votes, George W. Bush was decreed president of the United States. The senior senator from the state where the coal slurry spill occurred was overcome with glee. "I don't think I have ever felt better, including my own election victories, than the night of the Supreme Court decision," McConnell said later. "I felt so deeply that Al Gore was a horrible person and was wrong for the country and ought not to be president of the United States." As head of the Rules Committee, McConnell would preside over the inauguration, and inaugurating Gore, he said, would have been "enough to make me want to call in sick." Instead, Bush was sworn in at a $40 million ceremony. And that day, Tony Oppegard got a call in

Prestonsburg, Kentucky, from superiors at MSHA telling him that the incoming Bush administration was declining to approve the six-month extension that had been arranged for Oppegard so he could finish the investigation. "It was 'Don't come back tomorrow, because you're out of a job,' basically," he says.

Tim Thompson, a district manager from Morgantown, West Virginia, replaced Oppegard. On arriving in Kentucky, Thompson announced that he wanted the investigation scaled back. Spadaro and his colleagues still had thirty people left to interview, but he told them that they only had time for six. "We were told, 'Boys, you need to close out your investigation,'" says Spadaro. "We said, no, we're not done. He said, 'You're done.'"

Thompson says the investigation needed to be reined in because it was getting beyond issues of mine safety and into environmental violations better left to the EPA and state environmental officials. "Some of the environmental things were really ugly," he said. "But the violations they said existed were not violations of the Mine Safety Act." Spadaro and Oppegard disagreed, saying the violations they were pursuing were very much related to mine safety, given that the holding pond was next to a working coal mine.

There was a new regime at the Mine Safety and Health Administration. And at the top was Elaine Chao, Mitch McConnell's second wife, whom Bush nominated as secretary of labor upon taking office. Chao had suitable politics for the Bush administration (she was far more conservative than McConnell's first wife) but had little experience with mining safety. In addition to running the Peace Corps, she had led the United Way and served on the Federal Maritime Commission. Her husband, on the other hand, had for sixteen years represented one of the biggest coal mining states in the country. She turned to him to fill out her office. She hired as her chief of staff Steven Law, who had served six years as McConnell's chief of staff. She hired as her spokesman McConnell's former spokesman. Bush nominated as the head of MSHA a former Utah coal operator named David Lauriski; his two deputies were also former coal mining executives. Lauriski in turn hired as one of his aides yet another former McConnell staffer, Andrew Rajec, who started attending many of the meetings of the Martin County investigators.

Thompson pushed to have the case against Massey reduced to just two violations with a fine of $55,000 each, rather than the eight that Spadaro and his fellow investigators believed were justified. One day in April 2002, Thompson got a call from MSHA headquarters outside Washington, D.C., after which, with the investigators watching, he crossed out a section of the draft report that called MSHA to account for its lax oversight.

That was enough for Spadaro. Seeing where things were heading, he tendered his resignation in a letter published in the local papers. "I do not believe that the accident investigation report, as it is being developed, will offer complete and objective analysis of the accident and its causes," he wrote. As word of Spadaro's protest spread, Elaine Chao dismissed it by telling a reporter, "It's time to call off the MSHA food fight over the Martin County Coal Slurry investigation."

For Spadaro, the consequences for speaking out became clear. Back at his regular post running MSHA's training academy in West Virginia, he became the target of an internal audit for making thirteen cash advances with his agency credit card to entertain students and visiting dignitaries, including a Chinese delegation. He had paid the charges back, but the audit cited $22.60 in processing fees for the advances and suspended him for three days. In 2003, he was called to MSHA headquarters in Arlington, Virginia, and upbraided for letting an MSHA inspector with multiple sclerosis who was teaching classes at the academy live at the academy free of charge. Spadaro noted that his superiors had approved the arrangement, but he was placed on administrative leave anyway. He learned later that while he'd been in Arlington, MSHA officials had gone to his office in West Virginia to confiscate his files and hard drive. They picked apart his family photos to search for incriminating evidence he might have tucked inside the frames. A few months later, he was fired. He challenged his termination and had it reduced to administrative leave, but when the agency then demoted him and ordered him to a post in Pittsburgh, he relented and quit.

Meanwhile, the dispute over the Martin County investigation carried on in Spadaro's absence. In October 2001, Thompson asked that the remaining investigators sign off on the final report, without giving them a chance to read it. When they protested, Thompson put them on a conference call with Lauriski, the new MSHA chief, who made clear that the orders were coming from the top. The following April, MSHA cited Martin County Coal with just the two violations, and so halfhearted a case had the agency mounted for even those two that one was later overturned by an administrative judge and the other reduced to a mere $5,600.

The company did face $3.5 million in state fines, plus undisclosed restitution costs to homeowners. But the lightness of the repercussions from the main federal oversight agency for coal mines was conspicuous. In 2003, the Department of Labor's inspector general released a report on the investigation confirming most of Spadaro's claims about the undermining of the investigation by his superiors—but the impact of the report itself was softened by widespread redactions that left half of the twenty-six pages crossed out.

Why had Elaine Chao's Department of Labor gone so easy on Martin County Coal and Massey Energy? It would have been easy enough to blame the slurry spill on the Clinton administration, whose MSHA appointees had been so lax in following up on the recommendations following the 1994 spill.

Doing so, though, would've meant coming down hard on the coal industry—not just Massey Energy, but other coal companies as well, to the extent that the administration decided to tighten restrictions on the dozens of other slurry impoundments built over coal mines. And Elaine Chao and the rest of the administration were unlikely to take that approach. The coal industry had tripled its contributions in the 2000 campaign, more than four years earlier, and virtually all of this money had gone to Republicans. A coal tycoon whom Massey brought onto its board in 2001, James H. "Buck" Harless, had raised $275,000 for Bush's campaign, kicked in $5,000 for the Florida recount fight, and topped it off with $100,000 for the inaugural fund.

The financial bond was even stronger with the senator who had played such an influential role in filling the senior levels of Elaine Chao's administration. Yes, the residents who'd seen their property damaged and water contaminated by the slurry spill were Mitch McConnell's constituents. But over McConnell's career, his fifth-biggest source of campaign contributions was Peabody Energy, the largest coal company in the world. And between 1997 and 2000, when McConnell was leading the National Republican Senatorial Committee, the coal industry had given $584,000 to the group, making it one of the group's most reliable supporters, according to *Washington Monthly*.

Those contributions to the NRSC hadn't included any from Massey Energy. That is, not until 2002, with the investigation still proceeding, when Massey gave the NRSC $100,000. McConnell had over the prior decade also been the second-highest recipient in Washington of direct contributions from people tied to Massey, according to the Center for Responsive Politics.

Spadaro, for one, had no difficulty connecting the dots. "It was Mitch McConnell who fired Jack Spadaro," he says. "I've been around a long time and I swear this was one of the most outrageous things I've seen. It was one of the most blatant circumventions of the law and it was all orchestrated by Mitch McConnell's people."

———

It hadn't always been about the money, at least at first. In December 1973, while newly installed as chairman of the Jefferson County GOP at a time when the shadow of Watergate was lengthening over his party, the thirty-one-year-old McConnell had submitted an op-ed to the *Courier-Journal* calling for "truly effective campaign finance reform." His proposal was aggressive: in local Kentucky races, he said, contribution limits should be drastically lowered, from $2,500 to $300; all donors should be disclosed; and candidates should have to abide by a ceiling on overall spending—a restraint that many of the most aggressive of campaign finance reformers have been leery to propose. That wasn't all. He hailed a city-run campaign trust fund then under consideration and wrote favorably of public financing for both gubernatorial campaigns and presidential campaigns. Under the status quo, he lamented, "Many qualified and ethical persons are either totally priced out of the election marketplace or will not submit themselves to questionable, or downright illicit, practices that may accompany the current electoral process."

Years later, McConnell dismissed his op-ed as mere posturing, "playing for headlines" to divert readers from Watergate. To the extent his position was at all sincere, he said, he began to reassess it a few months later, while teaching a night class at the University of Louisville. Or as Dyche paraphrased it: "After studying and teaching how political parties operated and elections were won, he began to believe that much of what he had been saying about campaign finance was radically wrong. This epiphany would become an important part of his political philosophy and a focal point of his future career."

This was a charitable interpretation, that a single class as an adjunct instructor would bring about a transformation in how to judge the ethics of money in politics. McConnell had been around enough campaigns by that point to know "how elections were won." More credible was a different explanation that McConnell offered for his own evolution, one tied not to his 1974 class but to his first victory as a candidate, in 1977. The race against Hollenbach had been the most expensive race in Louisville's history. McConnell had spent $355,000 to win it. The lesson to the former reformer was plain: in campaigns, "[e]verything else is in second place" to fund-raising, he told the *Courier-Journal* after taking office. "Paid television commercials are an indispensable part of winning a modern campaign in an urban area. This is not to say that I like that or am happy about it, or that I think it's the most informed way to make a decision. It is nevertheless a fact of life." In the future, he warned any and all opponents, "I will always be well financed, and I'll be well financed early."

As grudging as this concession to reality sounded, Mitch McConnell seemed to *like* fund-raising—or at least liked it enough to excel at it. Joe Whittle, the former state Republican chairman who campaigned alongside McConnell in 1984, still marvels at his lack of reluctance when it came to asking others for money. "Mitch has an uncanny ability to sit down with people and tell them what needs to be done and say, 'I need your help.'" Whittle compared it to his own meager collection during his run for state attorney general. "A small-town lawyer like I was would ask for fifty dollars. He'd ask for five thousand." If, Whittle says, McConnell called someone up who told him, "I'm a little tight now. I'm going to wait till after the primary," McConnell refused to settle for that, knowing that the limit for giving after the primary was only half as much. "He'd say, 'There's a report coming out and I need to show support,'" says Whittle. Dyche recounts a time in McConnell's endless cold-calling of Republican donors in 1984 when he went to the wrong house and nonetheless finagled $4,000 out of the mistaken hosts, and $2,000 from their relative next door.

Former senator Alan Simpson, a Wyoming Republican who served alongside McConnell for twelve years, says this avidity was one of the most striking characteristics of McConnell. "When you raise the flag and somebody hollers from the back of the room, 'Does anyone want to go to a fund-raiser and raise some bucks?' Mitch will be right there," says Simpson. "It's a joy to him. He gets a twinkle in his eye and his step quickens. I mean, he loves it." Forgy, the Reagan campaign chairman in Kentucky, speculates that this strength derives from McConnell's recognition of his own weakness, the same self-awareness his first campaign consultants noted in him. "He knows that without a definite advantage in money, he's not going anywhere in politics. If he had to meet voters on a stump in a traditional way, the way politicians used to, without the benefit of ads, he'd be a lost ball in high weeds," Forgy says. "Politics in small Southern states requires a certain amount of showmanship and he just didn't have the ability to do that."

The ease of relieving supporters of their money extended beyond campaign contributions. On being elected county executive, which was paid about $80,000 in today's dollars, McConnell set up an arrangement with an undisclosed group of local business leaders who had supported his campaign. They paid a supplement of $25,000—$91,000 in today's dollars—in exchange for giving some speeches around town. "It had never been done before," says Hollenbach. "It was all kind of a mystery. Suddenly there was this mysterious group contributing $30,000 in matching funds." (Some reports put the sum at more than $30,000.) After his high-spending reelection campaign for county executive, McConnell had accepted a free five-day vacation to Cancun paid for by a Louisville television station as part of a promotion for heavy advertisers. The eagerness to accept supplementary income continued when he reached the Senate. Just two years after hammering Huddleston for his cross-country travel to give paid speeches, McConnell earned $10,500 during an eleven-day speaking tour on the West Coast. He reported the income but got unwelcome headlines later when it emerged that he had let corporate sponsors pay for his companion's travel expenses as well as his own, plus her expenses for an expensive trip to Japan, against Federal Election Commission rules. "Many of us are not millionaires," he said at the time, explaining his speechifying. "It's nice to have some options."

So adept was McConnell at fund-raising that, by his own admission, he spent a lot of his time in his first months in Washington devoted to it, five years before his next race—a level of preparation that at that point was still unusual among senators. By the end of 1985, he had banked more than $700,000 in today's dollars, "putting more emphasis on reelection than legislation," as Dyche put it.

Before too long, though, the fund-raising was becoming such an emphasis that it was not so much diverting McConnell from legislating as determining which legislation he cared about. In 1987, he sponsored a proposed constitutional amendment giving Congress the power to limit independent expenditures on campaigns and on candidates' use of personal funds for their own races. In May 1990, he made his first real reach out of junior-status obscurity when he wrote the Republican counterproposal to a sweeping Democratic campaign finance reform bill that would have instituted partial public financing for Senate and House candidates who agreed to voluntary spending limits. McConnell's plan rejected public financing and spending limits (both of which he'd spoken favorably of in that 1973 op-ed) and instead called for abolishing political action committees. The PAC clampdown had the benefit of both appearing principled and being self-interested: McConnell was still sore about having gotten less PAC support in 1984 than Huddleston had (though he'd risen in the ranks of PAC beneficiaries once in office).

But the real point of contention was spending limits. It looked for a while as if a compromise that included them was gaining ground among some Republican senators. At a GOP retreat in West Virginia, the rookie senator rose to quash this momentum, arguing that rejecting spending limits was, in the words of one participant, "in the best interest of Republicans." He rallied enough Republicans to sustain a filibuster against the compromise while, with his own proposal, having given his party cover on the issue. "Thus far he's devoted himself to coming up with proposals that make compromise impossible," said Oklahoma senator David Boren, the lead sponsor of the Democratic bill. "I really think he doesn't want to see a change in the current program, unless it works to the advantage of his own party."

McConnell had found his legislative calling. He was becoming informed enough on the dry subject to get more senior colleagues to listen to him. ("Like him or not, Mitch McConnell is an expert on campaign finance reform," veteran New Hampshire Republican Warren Rudman said in 1990.) And he was learning the art of opposing reforms that might hurt his party while at the same time supporting ones that would hurt the other party—or that stood no real chance of becoming law. In 1993, his focus shifted from banning PAC contributions to banning "soft money," the large sums collected by parties from corporations, unions, and wealthy donors outside the individual contribution limits for candidates, a source of funds that Democrats were becoming adept at exploiting for so-called issue ads that barely skirted prohibitions against the use of such funds to aid specific candidates directly. "Soft money should be banned. All campaign spending should be on the top of the table where voters can see it," McConnell wrote in a 1993 op-ed.

And he was discovering another tool of gamesmanship: how to gum up the works for partisan advantage. In 1994, as Democrats were trying to make the most of their remaining months before midterm elections that were boding poorly for them, McConnell deduced that the Senate would have to pass three motions, each subject to filibuster before the House and Senate could settle differences between the campaign finance bills passed by each chamber that year. In a kind of eureka moment, McConnell launched successful filibusters of these once-routine motions, thereby eating up much of the Democrats' precious remaining time on the calendar—and foiling campaign finance reform in the process. It was, he told the *Weekly Standard* years later, his "proudest legislative accomplishment" to date.

———

Once it takes hold, the motivating force of money in politics is boundless, reshaping and redirecting everything in its path, not unlike runaway coal slurry.

On arriving in the Senate in 1985, McConnell had been as-
signed, for the two committee seats allotted to each senator, to
serve on the Judiciary and Agriculture panels. Two years later, he
had switched from Judiciary to the esteemed Foreign Relations
Committee, following in the footsteps of John Sherman Cooper
and giving him a perch for his increasingly hawkish, international-
ist views. But in 1993, he leapt at the opportunity to leave Foreign
Relations for Appropriations, where, with the Republican takeover
of Congress in 1994, he assumed the chairmanship of the subcommittee on foreign operations.

This change was the best of both worlds—being able to keep
a hand in world affairs while also getting to have a hand on the
budget. Holding hearings and issuing reports at Foreign Relations
was one thing, but deciding which programs or countries got how
much of the country's $20 billion foreign aid budget was some-
thing else entirely. And it came with a crucial bonus: those with
control over the money tended to raise more money.

Some of the causes championed by the new subcommittee
chairman appeared to be the function of a genuine internation-
alism seeking to protect human rights and oppose communism.
Long before Aung San Suu Kyi became a global celebrity, McConnell promoted the plight of suppressed dissidents in Burma. But
it was hard not to notice that other small countries that attracted
McConnell's interest happened to be attached to ethnic communi-
ties in the United States eager to reward him for his efforts.

In the decade after he took control of the subcommittee, Mc-
Connell increased annual aid to the small former Soviet republic of
Armenia to $90 million a year, or as much as $25 million more than
the Clinton and Bush administrations sought. At the same time,
he took a cooler stance toward Azerbaijan, Armenia's neighbor and
historic rival, which has a far smaller immigrant community in the
United States. In 1992, he had been one of only four members of
Congress who voted to allow aid to Azerbaijan, but after taking over
the appropriations subcommittee, he turned against that nation

during its territorial disputes with Armenia, which resulted in more than a half-million refugees on the Azeri side of the border. By the late 1990s, Azerbaijan was receiving $12 per capita in U.S. aid, to Armenia's $180. And in 2004, McConnell touted this skewed arrangement in a speech to an Armenian-American conference in Washington. "Armenia received $75 million last year, and that is considerably more than Azerbaijan, an imbalance I don't apologize for," he said. "And we will try to achieve such an imbalance again this year."

The gratitude of Armenian-Americans—a famously cohesive immigrant community—was abundant. A wealthy Armenian-American bakery magnate, Albert Boyajian, who took McConnell on a tour of Armenia in 1996, hosted an annual fund-raiser in California for his "good friend Mitch." Armenian-Americans in California alone had given McConnell $125,000 after his first decade on the subcommittee, as the *Herald-Leader* noted in 2006. Boyajian himself gave $50,000 to Republicans over the prior decade, and was awarded the "Republican Senatorial Medal of Freedom" by the National Republican Senatorial Committee, which McConnell led for four years.

Confronted with these dollar figures by the *Herald-Leader*, McConnell downplayed their influence. "I assume they support myself and others because they like my views," he said then. But in 1996 he was more candid about his motivations, in remarks he made on the Senate floor. "We have a lot of Jewish-Americans who are interested in Israel, a lot of Armenian-Americans who are interested in Armenia, and a lot of Ukraine-Americans who are interested in Ukraine," he said. "Boy, when we hear from them, we get real interested." McConnell was speaking for himself—from his arrival in the Senate, he had built close ties to the American Israel Public Affairs Committee, and as subcommittee chairman, he had earmarked $225 million per year for Ukraine, for which he was rewarded on fund-raising trips to neighboring Ohio and Illinois, both home to large Ukrainian-American communities.

The dynamic was obvious. And it caused no end of difficulties for both the Clinton and George W. Bush administrations, since every dollar of foreign aid spent above an administration request for one country or group meant less for another. Fixed earmarks like the one for Ukraine left the administration with less flexibility to adapt to changing circumstances around the world. "He could go to places like Chicago and Cleveland and raise money. It was a big factor—and it was a factor in terms of our zero sum budget," says J. Brian Atwood, who served as Clinton's administrator of the U.S. Agency for International Development.

The administration had a sizable "peace dividend" to use after the Cold War and had been hoping to direct some of it to development in the Third World, but McConnell again and again would direct it to his favored nations instead. "He took it all out of USAID when he earmarked for these countries," says Atwood. "He not only created foreign policy issues for us but squeezed out money for other purposes." Atwood would protest this arrangement at McConnell's hearings, with "those cold, hard eyes" of McConnell staring down on him, to no avail. "He would smile wryly," Atwood recalls. "We all knew what the game was about."

———

The reach of money—and the pressure to raise it—was so broad that it encompassed even the realm of romance.

McConnell had started dating Elaine Chao in 1991, after being set up with her at a candlelight dinner arranged by an old friend of his, a former public-interest lawyer against the Vietnam War. (McConnell had prevailed over another suitor, President George H. W. Bush's White House counsel C. Boyden Gray, according to the *New York Times*.) At the time they were dating, Chao was the director of the Peace Corps, and McConnell's neighbors in Capitol Hill would see her pull up to pick him up in her official chauffeured town car. (When word of this use of the taxpayer-funded car got back to legislative staffers who handled the Peace Corps budget—on the subcommittee McConnell would later lead—they called the agency and demanded an explanation.)

But McConnell had known Chao and her family for a few years prior—as campaign contributors. When Chao had first met McConnell in 1987, she was serving on the Federal Maritime Commission, a natural posting for the daughter of a Chinese shipping magnate. James Chao had fled from mainland China to Taiwan in 1949, before coming to the United States a decade later, but had in recent years started doing more and more business with the mainland.

Chao had started raising money for Republicans while on the maritime commission, and in 1989 her family and associates' largesse began to flow to McConnell as well. Just days after the Chinese army killed several hundred protesters amid the Tiananmen Square uprising, McConnell received $10,000 from her family and others tied to her father's company, Foremost Maritime. A couple of months later, McConnell flew to a Los Angeles fund-raiser with Asian-Americans in the Pacific Leadership Conference, a group that included two people who would later be convicted of laundering political contributions for Democratic candidates. That event netted McConnell $10,750, which brought his total 1989 take from this new source of contributors to $21,750—not all that much less, the *New Republic* noted in a 2001 article, than the $32,500 he had netted that year from his top backers at the time, tobacco PACs.

The subsequent shift in McConnell's approach to China was even more marked than his evolution on the Armenia-Azerbaijan conflict. On arriving in the Senate, his rush to show his conservative bona fides had included allying himself with Jesse Helms, the stridently anticommunist ranking Republican on the Foreign Relations Committee. In McConnell's first year, he had joined just seven Republicans to sign a fiery letter from Helms demanding that the Reagan administration name more hawks to top foreign policy positions. Helms's brand of conservatism translated into fierce opposition of the Chinese government, and on the rare occasions when McConnell spoke out about China, he adopted a bellicose tone.

As the contributions started coming in, McConnell's interest in China grew and his tone softened. He helped win a special provision that the members of the Pacific Leadership Conference were seeking, a fourfold increase in the number of annual visas for Hong Kong residents. He also adopted another goal of many in the Chinese-American business community, the opening of the Chinese economy. And he came around to supporting "most favored nation" status for China, without conditions—a major break with Helms. As the economic ties expanded and the Chinese economy boomed, so did McConnell's standing with the companies thriving off the growth: in the two years prior to his 1996 reelection, the *New Republic* reported, he received PAC contributions from 19 of the top 20 contributors of the U.S.-China Business Council. James Chao—as of 1993, his father-in-law—remained generous, raising $34,000 for McConnell in the month in 1994 when he took the helm of the Senate's Foreign Operations subcommittee. In 1996, the Chao family added $25,000 for the Kentucky Republican Party. (None of this activity kept McConnell from warning about "Red China" in fund-raising letters attacking the Clinton administration for the murky campaign money it received from Asian donors in 1996.)

Back in 1989, in the wake of the Tiananmen Square massacre, McConnell had declared that he would "never forget the sight of those young people without arms up against tanks and machine guns." But as the next decade progressed, the ties grew ever closer with the regime that had ordered that crackdown. The Chinese representative to the United Nations was a guest at McConnell and Chao's wedding. Later that year, the newlyweds went to Beijing with James Chao, and McConnell became only the second Republican senator to meet with Chinese leader Jiang Zemin since the 1989 massacre. Jiang met again with the couple when he came to Washington in 1997. And in 1999, McConnell and Chao hosted the Chinese ambassador at the University of Louisville, where the ambassador railed against the U.S. House of Representatives for having condemned his government's violent suppression of the Falun Gong religious sect, comments that McConnell made no attempt to distance himself from in his own remarks. Harry Wu, who spent about twenty years in Chinese prisons as a political dissident before landing at the Hoover Institution, a conservative think tank, told the *Herald-Leader* what motivated McConnell's warming relations with Beijing: "No mystery. It's the money."

The University of Louisville itself became a focus of the growing McConnell bond with China. In 1991, at the start of his second term and as his relationship with Chao and his ties to Chinese-Americans donors were building, McConnell began setting up what would become the McConnell Center for Political Leadership at his alma mater, essentially a scholarship program for young Kentuckians interested in political science that also hosts occasional lectures and visits by dignitaries. From the start, there was a strong Chinese inflection at the center—scholarship recipients were expected to spend a summer in China, and a disproportionate share of the center's events involved China, such as the ambassador's anti–Falun Gong speech.

Given that the focus of such ventures often reflects the interests of the funders, it was natural to wonder whether the center was getting support from some of the same Chinese-American donors who had started donating to McConnell's campaigns in the same period. But there was no way of knowing. The McConnell Center, for which McConnell raised $2.4 million at the outset and another $1 million or so over the course of the next decade, was not going to disclose its donors, a condition that the University of Louisville faculty affiliated with the center were not happy with, but accepted as an unconditional requirement from McConnell. "We made a little pact with the devil," says Ron Vogel, the former chairman of the university's political science department, now a professor at Ryerson University in Toronto. "We had a discussion: Do we want to have a McConnell Center? If we're going to have one, the money had to be raised for it, and if he's going to go out and raise the money, he's not going to want us sniping about it."

The faculty decided to go along with it, and McConnell got a big boon: the publicity that came from the perennial photo ops he'd take with each year's ten scholarship recipients and from the events with the visiting dignitaries, all under the aegis of a program named for him. There were occasional conflicts, such as the time in the late 1990s when one of the scholarship recipients became pregnant, to McConnell's great anger. He proposed a new requirement that recipients not have any children, a suggestion opposed by the faculty, who argued that the program should be supportive of a young woman who decided to carry a child to term, and should not be engaged in administering chastity oaths. Over time, though, the odds of such conflicts diminished as McConnell shifted the center out of the control of the faculty, with leadership of his choosing.

All throughout, McConnell and allied administrators at the university fought to keep the center's donors secret. When the *Courier-Journal* sued for disclosure, the case climbed all the way to the state Supreme Court, which in 2008 ruled that future donors would have to be disclosed but that the center's sixty-two donors to that point could remain hidden. The *Courier-Journal* had managed to suss out some of the past donors—$833,000 from Toyota (which counted McConnell among its Washington allies during the storm over its massive 2010 recall); $600,000 combined from R. J. Reynolds and Philip Morris; and $250,000 from Yum! Inc., the huge KFC/Pizza Hut/Taco Bell franchiser, which stood to benefit from a bill sponsored by McConnell to protect the fast-food industry against lawsuits charging that their offerings cause obesity, heart disease, and diabetes.

Perhaps most notable, though, was the $500,000 gift for the center from a subsidiary of BAE Systems, the giant British-based defense contractor, which in 2010 paid a record $450 million fine to settle an extended bribery investigation by American and British authorities. In 2007, with that investigation already public knowledge, McConnell secured for BAE three earmarks worth $25 million—for purchases that the Pentagon itself had not requested.

It was just what some of the university's faculty members had warned about at the outset. "We didn't want this to become a mechanism for influence peddling outside normal channels for political accountability," says one professor. "We were concerned about who would be funding it and that the department would be implicated in postures we wouldn't even know about because we wouldn't know who the funders were." Vogel, the former political science department chairman, was more fatalistic: "What money supporting these things has ever been clean?"

––––––––

One day in 1995, McConnell was huddling in the Senate with one of his few confidants, Robert Bennett of Utah, when he told him he was about to flip on a hot-button issue. Back in 1990, McConnell had joined most of his fellow Republicans in voting for an amendment to ban flag-burning—and had then proceeded to attack Harvey Sloane in that fall's campaign over his party's opposition to the amendment. But with Bennett's fellow Utah Republican, Orrin Hatch, mounting a new push for an amendment five years later, McConnell was ready to join only three other Republicans in opposing it—Bennett and two liberal New Englanders, John Chafee and James Jeffords. As Bennett recalls, "He said, 'You know, I voted for it and just as I walked off the floor I realized I made a mistake. And I'm not going to vote to weaken the First Amendment ever again.'"

If one needed further proof of how central money in politics had become for McConnell, this flip-flop was it: he was willing to surrender a perennial crowd-pleasing issue to strengthen his case for arguing against limits on campaign financing. Up until this point, McConnell had relied on expedient arguments to make his case against new regulations, pointing out to his fellow Republicans how this or that new rule would hurt their party or help the other party. He was no less blunt in justifying his opposition to campaign finance restrictions to the reformers and editorialists who chided him for it, arguing that Kentucky Republicans had no choice but to rake in as much money as they could if they wanted to compete in a state with so many more registered Democrats and with its two major newspapers, the *Courier-Journal* and *Herald-Leader,* leaning left. Money, he said, was the great leveler.

But this justification was growing thinner. Kentucky still had more registered Democrats than Republicans, but it was trending toward the latter, especially in federal elections—1996 would be the last time a Democratic presidential candidate carried the state. Eventually the state would be down to a single Democratic congressman out of six. McConnell's case for fighting restrictions would be far stronger if it could be lashed to a constitutional principle, namely the First Amendment's protection of freedom of speech. In *Buckley v. Valeo,* its landmark decision on campaign finance, the Supreme Court had ruled that the First Amendment barred limits on political spending, while leaving some room for the government to regulate direct contributions to candidates. This ruling, in 1976, had not kept McConnell from maintaining his support for various levels of restrictions for more than a decade—including that constitutional amendment he proposed in 1987 to circumvent *Buckley*'s interpretation of the First Amendment. Two decades later, though, he saw the power of the First Amendment claim in *Buckley.* To make his resistance to stricter regulations credible, he knew it would help to be seen as standing on that principle. There was no better way to stake a claim to principle than to hew to it even when it went against one of his party's political planks: the prohibition of flag-burning.

It was shrewd. McConnell got great symbolic weight out of surrendering a political gambit—an amendment to ban flag-burning—that was never going to be more than symbolic itself.

It was cost-free, with a huge payoff (and to make sure it was cost-free, McConnell cosponsored a separate, fig-leaf bill calling for the protection of the flag). "He switched to the First Amendment," says Joan Claybrook, who often faced off against McConnell on campaign finance reform in her long tenure as president of Public Citizen. "It was pure politics—whatever rationale sold, he would use. I don't think he believed it for a minute." Even those far more sympathetic to McConnell suspect that his free speech invocations had more than a little expedience in them: "He believes in freedom of speech, but as a pragmatic politician he also believes in the power of political spending," says Richard Lugar, the former Republican senator from Indiana who was one of McConnell's closest associates. "Pragmatically, he's come to the conclusion that raising money is tremendously important for his own success."

An added bonus in McConnell's newfound consistency in standing up for the First Amendment was that it provided cover for his continued inconsistency on the particulars of campaign finance law. Just as he had abandoned his support for spending limits and in its place proposed banning soft money, the unlimited contributions that flowed to parties from corporations, unions, and wealthy individuals, as the decade went on McConnell started taking up the defense of soft money, calling it preferable to undisclosed spending by outside groups. "Soft money is just a euphemism for free speech," he said. The shift could be explained, again, by changing circumstances: back when McConnell had proposed soft money clampdowns in 1993, it appeared Democrats had the edge with soft money. (Claybrook still recalls bringing along a chart to show McConnell at hearings, to persuade him out of his conviction that Democrats were benefiting more from soft money than Republicans.)

But after the soft money scandals of the 1996 election, which involved illegal foreign money and the use of the Lincoln Bedroom in the White House, the reformers' attention turned to reining in those funds—and who should rise in opposition but McConnell. By that point, the truth of Claybrook's claim about the Republicans benefiting no less from soft money than Democrats had become harder to deny. ("If we stop this thing, we can control the institution for the next twenty years," McConnell reportedly told Republican colleagues in 1997, referring to the effort to ban soft money.) And McConnell had himself become a crucial cog in the party machinery that relied so much on soft money, by having become, in 1997, the head of the National Republican Senatorial Committee. As efforts to limit soft money gained momentum late in the decade—led by the bipartisan duo of Arizona Republican John McCain and Wisconsin Democrat Russ Feingold—the first line of resistance to them was the author of an op-ed from just a few years earlier arguing for that very reform.

From his new perch as chairman of the Senate Rules Committee, McConnell would parry endlessly with the advocates of greater restrictions on soft money who would appear before him at hearings and who, almost in spite of themselves, came to respect his grasp of the subject. "He did not seem to be reading off of a script like everybody else is," says Joshua Rosenkranz, a lawyer who, as then-president of the Brennan Center for Justice, came before the committee arguing for restrictions on outside spending on elections in the final weeks before Election Day. "It was one of the more intellectual exchanges I've had on Capitol Hill in a world where intellectual exchanges are quite rare." It was striking watching the dour senator come alive on this issue, Rosenkranz says. "There is passion there—it is real and palpable," he says. "Whether it's passion driven by a philosophy of what the Constitution should permit in a free society or passion driven by a desire to enable his side to win elections, I just don't know."

McConnell took his cause everywhere. He started enlisting conservative talk radio, notably Rush Limbaugh's show, to talk up his cause. He became a regular on the networks and cable TV—in 1999, he made ninety-nine appearances on national television. In addition to rallying conservative think tanks and editorialists behind his cause, he reached out to the American Civil Liberties

Union, realizing that having that liberal group on his side would only buttress his claim to be fighting spending restrictions on constitutional and not partisan grounds. The ACLU, which at the time viewed contribution limits as a restriction on free speech (it has since rethought that stance), acquiesced. "McConnell wanted to make use of our opposition, and we did not mind," says Laura Murphy, head of the ACLU's Washington legislative office. "He developed a healthy respect for our organization and our principled stand." McConnell also crossed the aisle within the Senate, framing his anti-reform arguments in ways he knew might connect with some Democrats. He showed up at the office of Bob Kerrey, the Nebraska Democrat, to try to get him to drop his support for limited public campaign financing. McConnell knew Kerrey fancied himself an entitlement reformer, so that's how he pitched this case: "He came and made a case that public finance is creating a new entitlement," Kerrey recalls. "I had spent a lot of time on entitlements, so he almost persuaded me to be with him."

On the flip side, McConnell punished fellow Republicans pushing for new campaign finance restrictions. In 1998, he withheld funding from the National Republican Senatorial Committee for the campaign of Linda Smith, a Washington congresswoman who was challenging Democratic senator Patty Murray. Smith was a staunch conservative who had fought to cut government spending and limit abortions, but she also favored getting special interest money out of politics. Dale Foreman, then the chairman of the Washington State Republican Party, recalls meeting with McConnell in his Senate office to find out what sort of support the NRSC would provide to unseat Murray and hearing the unvarnished warning: if Linda Smith got the nomination, her support for campaign finance reform would keep the NRSC out of the race. "He was very lukewarm on her candidacy," says Foreman. "It was very clear that he did not want Linda Smith to be the nominee for the state of Washington and if she was, he was not in favor of using national money to support her candidacy." McConnell held true to his word. Smith was left to fend for herself, and Murray won reelection easily.

Linda Smith was not the only natural ally to face repercussions for backing campaign finance reform. In the wake of the campaign funding scandals of the 1996 election, the Committee for Economic Development, an alliance of centrist business leaders, started exploring possible reforms to a system that encouraged cronyism and forced them to entertain constant entreaties for campaign money. "We prefer to compete in the marketplace, not the political realm," says Charles Kolb, the organization's then president. "People didn't like the shakedown." In 1999, the committee put out a report on the issue. When CNN did a segment on it, it introduced the news with a video of a man biting a dog, to convey the unlikeliness of big businesses speaking out against corporate money in politics. "We were going against the conventional wisdom: it was, 'Wait a minute, there are people in business who don't like the system?'" says Kolb. "We were challenging that, and saying that [the status quo] was a bad thing for the country, a bad thing for the economy, and a bad thing for the business community."

Not long after the report appeared, several of the committee's board members got a letter from the chairman of the National Republican Senatorial Committee, Mitch McConnell, asking them, in Kolb's words, "How could you of all people be associated with an organization that is in bed with radical environmentalists?" It was so "crudely" written, Kolb says, that the business leaders who received it assumed it had been drafted by an overzealous NRSC staff member, and disregarded it. But soon afterward, a second set of letters arrived on the same letterhead. This time there was no doubt of its provenance: at the bottom of the letters was a handwritten note from McConnell himself saying, essentially, "I hope you will resign from the CED."

Kolb was taken aback. He had a friendly history with McConnell—he had served as general counsel at the United Way under Elaine Chao's leadership, had gone with his wife out to dinner with

McConnell and Chao, and had contributed to McConnell's Senate campaign. And he did not understand why McConnell was so protective of the flawed status quo. "There's a strong conservative case to be made in favor of campaign finance reform," Kolb says. "I thought conservatives were in favor of the market as opposed to rent-seeking within the system."

The showdown made its way onto the front page of the *New York Times*. It drew some sympathetic business leaders and foundations to CED, but also cost it one major member, BellSouth. When Kolb asked an executive from the company why it was stopping its contributions to CED, he said: "Senator McConnell is a very important senator to this company."

At around the same time, McConnell made an even more direct challenge of the reform camp, on the floor of the Senate, setting off one of the chamber's more remarkable exchanges in modern history. On October 14, 1999, he dared John McCain to elaborate on his general argument that the money flooding campaigns was corrupting Washington. "For there to be corruption, someone must be corrupt," McConnell said. "I just ask my friend from Arizona what he has in mind here?"

McCain was easy to rile, but here he declined the bait. "I refuse to . . . say that any individual or person is guilty of corruption in a specific way," he said. The problem was more diffuse than that, he said. "There is a pernicious effect of money on the legislative process," he argued. "I am attacking a system. I am attacking a system that has to be fixed. . . . This system makes good people do bad things. . . . All of us are corrupted by it because money buys access and access is influence."

McConnell kept up the taunting. "How," he asked, "can it be corruption if no one is corrupt? That is like saying the gang is corrupt but none of the gangsters are. If there is corruption, someone must be corrupt."

McCain held firm. "That is not right. It is a system. It is a system that has violated the process and has therefore caused the American people to lose confidence and trust in the government." At one point, he finally turned on McConnell, though without naming him, as he cited as one example of generalized corruption McConnell's reassurance to other senators about voting against McCain's antismoking bill a year earlier: "A certain senator stood up and said it was okay for you not to vote for the tobacco bill because the tobacco companies will run ads in our favor."

Afterward, as McCain's campaign for the Republican presidential nomination was getting off the ground, McCain ran into Charles Kolb at a luncheon. They got to discussing McConnell, and Kolb mentioned the dinner that he and his wife had been to with McConnell and Chao years earlier. After being quiet at first, McConnell had opened up and been perfectly pleasant.

While he was relaying this story, Kolb says, McCain was gritting his teeth. "I haven't," McCain said when Kolb finished, "been privileged to see that side of him."

———

The rivalry resolved itself in a great victory for McCain. Or at least so it seemed at the time. For all of McConnell's maneuvering, he was unable to turn back the pro-reform tide that swelled amid the corporate scandals that followed the bursting of the tech-stock bubble, notably the 2001 collapse of Enron. That company had blanketed Capitol Hill with nearly $2 million in contributions over the previous four years. In the spring of 2002, the Senate passed the McCain-Feingold law—formally the Bipartisan Campaign Reform Act of 2002—and Bush signed it into law. McConnell stood against it until the end, warning in a *New York Times* op-ed ("In Defense of Soft Money") that the legislation "will not take any money out of politics. It just takes the parties out of politics," and in a floor speech of a "brave new world where the voices of parties are quieted, the voices of billionaires are enhanced, the voices of newspapers are enhanced."

But McConnell's seemingly lonely resistance had come with an invaluable consolation prize: the lasting gratitude of his fellow Republican senators. He hadn't exactly been embraced by his colleagues from the outset—he had, after all, lost in his first two bids to run the NRSC. But for the better part of a decade, he had made himself the face of opposition to reforms that he believed, and many others in the GOP Senate caucus agreed, would work to their party's detriment. Speaking up on behalf of the right to give and spend unlimited sums from corporate donors was not something most politicians were eager to do, but Mitch McConnell had taken up the task. And for that, his colleagues owed him a debt beyond what they'd already incurred from his prodigious fund-raising at the helm of the NRSC. "McConnell was not yet a leader [of the Republican caucus], and here he was protecting a lot of people by taking the heat," says Scott Harshbarger, who led Common Cause at the time and had previously served as attorney general of Massachusetts. "McConnell instinctively saw an opportunity to be an opposition force—he became the shield."

Not only that, but McConnell's stand against campaign finance reform raised a profile otherwise lacking in a legislative focus. Where McConnell was once but one in a crowd of new Republican senators from the South, he was now the notorious adversary of McCain and his admirers in the liberal media. And he relished it—after being branded the "Darth Vader" of money in politics, he once brought a light saber to a press conference. Taking up the fight "was a very smart political move," says Harshbarger. "Behind it may have been high principle, but at the time, it made his mark, and he had a lot of chits coming out of it. Otherwise, as a person he had no presence that would attract leadership—he was a milquetoast kind of guy. Before he got demonized, it was, 'Who the hell was Mitch McConnell?'"

Best of all, the downside was minimal. As much as McConnell liked to cast his opposition as an unpopular stand for principle, he knew that campaign finance reform was not an issue that excited voters back home. As he liked to say, "It ranks right up there with static cling as one of the great concerns among the American people." If anything, getting attacked by the *New York Times* and liberal activists for his opposition to reform was only helping McConnell strengthen his standing with conservative voters in Kentucky who might otherwise be wary of him. When Ellen Miller, a leader of the campaign finance reform movement, organized ads against McConnell in Kentucky attacking him for his opposition to McCain-Feingold, it backfired, recalls Harshbarger: "It got him only bigger margins."

McConnell did not drop the crusade with the passage of the law. Wasting no time, he led the move to challenge its constitutionality in court, and in 2003, the Supreme Court heard *McConnell v. Federal Election Commission*. A few months later, a slender 5–4 majority ruled for upholding most of the law. McConnell called it the "worst Supreme Court decision since the *Dred Scott* case"—a declaration that overlooked plenty of historically dubious rulings, such as *Korematsu v. United States* (1944), justifying the mass internment of 110,000 Japanese-Americans without individual cause, and *Plessy v. Ferguson* (1896), upholding a Louisiana law requiring the racial segregation of railway passengers.

Redemption came six years later, in 2010, with another 5–4 ruling by a reconfigured Supreme Court. *Citizens United v. Federal Election Commission* eviscerated restrictions on campaign spending by corporations, unions, and nonprofit groups, ruling that the free speech rights that allowed independent campaign spending by individuals applied to corporations as well. It did not overturn McCain-Feingold, per se—unlimited "soft money" for parties was still barred—but together with a string of other court and regulatory rulings it rendered the law increasingly irrelevant and vulnerable to dismantling by future court decisions.

Following the ruling, spending on elections by outside groups surged to $300 million in 2010, more than quadruple the previous midterm election, and to more than $1 billion in 2012, triple what it had been in 2008. This surge gave McConnell the chance to declare himself vindicated over his earlier warning that McCain-Feingold's bar on soft money would only shift the big money into "shadowy groups with innocuous-sounding names" outside the purview of the two major political parties, thereby weakening those institutions and empowering deep-pocketed fringe groups or individuals. This claim was valid, but only to a point—the boom in outside spending would not have been as great had the Supreme Court, in a ruling McConnell celebrated, not liberated outside groups to spend so freely on elections.

Moreover, McConnell and his party were not exactly holding back from capitalizing on the new free-for-all he had warned against early in the decade. The largest outside group to rise to prominence after the ruling was American Crossroads, an organization with deep ties to the Republican establishment. Its co-founder was Karl Rove, and its president was Steven Law, the former chief of staff to both McConnell and Elaine Chao, who had subsequently also worked with the U.S. Chamber of Commerce. In a sense, Crossroads offered an ideal combination to the Republican establishment in Washington—even if it was not allowed to coordinate directly with candidates, with Law at the helm it could be counted on to adopt strategies in line with the party leadership in Washington; at the same time, the group could accept far larger contributions than candidates, the party, or party committees like the NRSC could.

Even better, the contributions to American Crossroads' sister organization, Crossroads GPS, did not have to be disclosed, as it was classified as a 501(c)(4) nonprofit group, ostensibly more focused on "social welfare" than elections. This designation made Crossroads GPS a more appealing target for publicity-shy donors—while the regular Crossroads group raised $50 million for the 2012 campaign, GPS raised $123 million, $22.5 million of which came from a single anonymous donor. "I wouldn't want to discount the value of confidentiality to some donors," said Law in 2010.

The rise in undisclosed contributions raised questions reminiscent of the Watergate era. The Nixon White House had rustled up millions in secret donations from major companies worried they'd get hit with a tax audit or other penalty if they didn't give. Once again, with Crossroads GPS and similar groups, vast sums were trading hands without the public's knowledge. But that was only half the problem—while the public didn't know who was giving what, the people giving and receiving the money most certainly did, and so, presumably, did others in the party network in Washington. This combination of private disclosure and public nondisclosure gave enormous leverage to the fund-raisers: a company or individual approached for funds knew that if they rejected the advance, word might well get back to elected officials in Washington who would have sway over matters of importance to the company or individual; further raising the pressure was the fact that the targeted donor had no way of knowing whether his or her company's business rivals were or were not giving themselves.

With disclosure, one could at least attempt to connect the dots and hold elected officials accountable. In late 2012, lawmakers on Capitol Hill slipped language into the big "fiscal cliff" deal that gave biotech giant Amgen another two years before a kidney dialysis drug it makes would be subject to price controls—a tweak that would cost Medicare an estimated $500 million. Reporting on the added language, the *New York Times* noted that Amgen had close ties with Mitch McConnell, along with other senior lawmakers. Its employees had contributed $73,000 to him since 2007, including at a fund-raising event for him that Amgen helped sponsor while the fiscal cliff deal was being crafted, and its lobbyists included another of McConnell's former chiefs of staff.

But there was no similar accountability to be done with "social welfare" groups such as Crossroads GPS, since the identity of its donors was secret. Who was to say if Amgen had given heavily to that organization in 2012? Or, to take another example: somehow a budget implementation bill in 2012 wound up including a tax provision that threatened to quash the growing roll-your-own-cigarette industry. Who was to know if tobacco companies had given to Crossroads GPS and thus raised their odds of getting that language added? There was no way of knowing if that happened. Or if it didn't.

Even as his position on spending limits or PACs or soft money shifted, McConnell had spoken in favor of public disclosure of political giving and spending. It had become his ultimate mantra: stop trying to limit the inevitable flow of money into campaigns, but just make sure it's all out in the open. "Disclosure is the best disinfectant, and I think the maximum amount of disclosure is exactly what we need," he said on a Sunday morning show in 1996. Given how much concern he'd continued to express about unaccountable spending outside the party structure, it seemed natural that McConnell would continue to insist on disclosure of those outside dollars.

Even that last plank fell away. In 2010 Senate Democrats introduced the Disclose Act, legislation that would have forced outside groups spending more than $10,000 on campaign-related expenditures to disclose contributors who had donated more than $10,000. It was, says Norman Ornstein, a congressional scholar at the American Enterprise Institute, the "last best hope for doing anything to ameliorate *Citizens United.*" McConnell held together his caucus—even John McCain—for a successful filibuster of the bill. McConnell explained his reversal on disclosure by arguing that the bill favored unions and that the increasingly toxic political atmosphere put a new premium on protecting the privacy of major donors against what he called "liberal thugs." To one Senate Democrat who had supported the bill, McConnell's opposition to disclosure after years of speaking in favor of it was remarkable. "It's startling how flexible some people are in their opinions," he said. "For him, it's a matter of political convenience."

As with his previous shifts, though, this maneuver could also be explained by changing circumstances in the partisan landscape. The biggest spending by outside groups, by far, was being spent on the right, by groups such as Americans for Prosperity, which is backed by the billionaire Koch brothers, and the Crossroads network, which raised more than $70 million for the Republican sweep in 2010, more than any other group. This had prompted an admission of gratitude from McConnell for Crossroads' assistance: "We had a better day than we otherwise would have in 2010." As McConnell's campaign was gearing up in late 2013 for his sixth Senate race, Crossroads—with his former chief of staff, Steven Law, still at the helm—announced it would spend heavily to keep McConnell in power. "It certainly is personal to me," Law told the *Herald-Leader.*

With the barrels of anonymously donated money waiting to be unloaded in Kentucky, promise of even greater resources arrived with another Supreme Court ruling in the spring of 2014. In *McCutcheon v. Federal Election Commission,* the court was now eliminating the limits on how much donors could give overall in direct contributions to candidates, party committees, and political action committees in a given year. The decision was sweet indeed for McConnell—it was another blow to the underpinnings of McCain-Feingold, and Chief Justice John Roberts's argument against big money being corrupting echoed McConnell's challenge of McCain on the Senate floor years earlier.

Best of all, the ruling was expected to bring disproportionately more money into the coffers of Republican candidates, and no one was in a better position than McConnell to reach out to donors who'd be liberated by the lifting of the caps on overall giving. "There's nobody who gives money to Republicans that he doesn't know," says Bruce Lunsford, his 2008 opponent, in only a slight hyperbole. These additional funds would even have the sheen of legitimacy that the outside money would not, as the identities of donors would be disclosed. But for corporations or donors who still wanted to give secretly, there were still the outside groups waiting open-armed.

It was the best of both worlds.

———

In Inez, the traces of the Martin County Coal slurry spill are still everywhere. The embankment along meandering Coldwater Creek, once lined with cherry and walnut trees, now stands denuded and crumbling. One doesn't have to dig deep in spots along the creek to turn up the dark goop. Residents who once grew vegetables in their backyards dare not to anymore, for fear of what was left behind. Linc Chapman has lost about half the distance from the creek to his house. The company was supposed to pay to restore the embankment, but nothing came of it. The creek itself runs far emptier of fish than it did before October 11, 2000, so much so that Chapman was gladdened to see a couple of redhorse suckers darting along one day in April. The "creek bed reconstruction expert" from Colorado hired for the cleanup had assured residents that "you'll have trout swimming in these streams in two years," to which Chapman had thought at the time: "You are so full of shit." And indeed, aquatic life is just about "nonexistent" today, he says. "We had a lot of crawfish, freshwater eels, large-mouth bass, small-mouth, rock bass, blue-gill, channel cats, used to have a big run of quillback, they're like a sucker. They suck in sand and fill it to their gills, and it's hard to suck slurry through the gills." All are pretty much gone.

Farther up Coldwater Creek, one can still make out the lines on the trees that are still standing, showing how high the slurry climbed. Chapman also points out the uninhabited areas along the creek where the company dug big unlined pits to bury the sludge, with a thin layer of regular fill from the surrounding hills spread over the top of it. Some of the sludge was later dug back up and moved to proper disposal, but much of it remains. "As long as I live, there'll still be the impacts of it here," he says.

Chapman's family still doesn't trust the local water—it bathes and washes with it, but drinks only bottled water, as do many of the townspeople, or at least those who can afford it. The reservoir just outside Inez is fed by water from the Tug River, the main stem into which the contaminated Coldwater and Wolf Creeks flow. Chapman and others argued for requiring the company to pay for an independent monitor of the water quality, to no avail. "They were all for monitoring but wanted to do it in-house. Well, that's as useless as tits on a boar hog," he says. "If they pulled a sample from the bottom of the reservoir, they'd find a foot of slurry." No one's monitoring it now, in-house or otherwise. "It's one of those things where, after so much time that's what big companies hope, that it's out of sight, out of mind," Chapman says. "When you've got the government in your pockets, you get by with what you want to get by with."

The mine itself sits fallow, with only some reclamation work being done. It's now owned by Alpha Natural Resources, which in 2011 subsumed Massey Energy following an eventful decade for the company. In 2004, one year after Martin County Coal got only a small fine from MSHA, Massey CEO Don Blankenship spent more than $3 million to help elect a conservative Republican for the Supreme Court of Appeals of West Virginia, the state's highest court, paying for ads that accused the incumbent judge of being soft on child molesters and drug dealers. Once on the court, the new judge provided the decisive vote to overturn a $55 million judgment against Massey—a turn of events so glaring that the U.S. Supreme Court later ruled that the judge should have recused himself.

On April 5, 2010, nearly a decade after the Martin County spill, an explosion at Massey's Upper Big Branch mine in West Virginia killed twenty-nine miners. Investigators later found that Massey had allowed explosive methane and coal dust to build up to the point where it was ignited by a spark from a poorly maintained coal-cutting machine, producing a blast that clogged water sprayers were unable to suppress. Massey had covered up lethal safety violations, tipped off mine supervisors to inspections, and manipulated ventilation equipment and machinery to dupe inspectors.

Through it all, McConnell's ties to the coal industry have only grown stronger. Requests under the Freedom of Information Act for correspondence between McConnell and the Department of Labor during the eight years the department was run by his wife show repeated entreaties from the senator on behalf of mining companies, including Massey, complaining about excessive enforcement efforts by safety inspectors and new rules on miners' exposure to diesel particulate matter. One complaint about a $250,000 fine forwarded to federal regulators by McConnell makes its political appeal explicit: "I am a Registered Republican and need your help."

In late 2002, at the time as he was wrapping up the MSHA investigation in Martin County that would leave Massey unscathed, Tim Thompson had a meeting back at his office in Morgantown with another coal executive, Bob Murray, to discuss safety issues at one of Murray Energy's mines in Ohio. Murray, an obstreperous former miner, had brought a whole entourage with him in what Thompson saw as a deliberate show of force. As tensions rose in the close-packed room, Murray turned to Thompson and said: "Mitch McConnell calls me one of the five finest men in America, and the last I checked, he was sleeping with your boss," according to notes of the meeting obtained in 2003 by West Virginia Public Radio. "They," he added, pointing at two MSHA men whom he'd been dealing with over the safety issues, "are gone."

Thompson now says that he was not intimidated by Murray's remark: "I don't get too scared. I don't overreact," he says. "His mine was in Ohio, I was in West Virginia, and McConnell is in neither of those states." But his MSHA superiors in fact transferred Thompson to another region, away from Murray's mines, as was one of the other MSHA men at the meeting. Murray offered a suggestive response to the *Herald-Leader* in 2006 when asked about Thompson's transfer: "I said he should be removed. But they didn't do it because I said so."

Thompson fought the transfer for several years before giving up and retiring. At some point, McConnell's chief of staff contacted Thompson via a coal industry lawyer and asked for a statement on what happened at the meeting. Worried about any hard feelings with McConnell over the disclosure of Murray's comments regarding Chao, Thompson complied. "I wrote to say, 'Mitch McConnell had nothing to say or influence it, that Murray was acting like a renegade.'" The reason for the request was plain to Thompson: "My guess was there could've been some bad publicity that they tried to nip."

In 2007, Murray Energy suffered its own large-scale disaster: a collapse at its mine in Crandall Canyon in Utah, which claimed the lives of six miners and three rescuers. Bob Murray has been one of the most valued fund-raisers for Republicans in Washington—since 2007 alone, national Republicans have received more than $1 million from Murray, his family, and his salaried employees, who, documents show, were pressured to attend fund-raisers with visiting Republicans and contribute to the company PAC.

Murray's financial commitment ratcheted up as the threats to the Appalachian coal industry mounted. The industry was facing growing competition from cheap natural gas acquired through fracking, but Murray declared that its primary threat was the Obama administration's push to reduce carbon emissions. McConnell took this tack with increasing stridence as well. "The president may as well call his war on coal what it is: a war on jobs in this country, and a plan to ship jobs overseas," he said in 2013.

That a senator from a coal-producing state should take up this cry is not surprising. Still, it rung hollow. Coal wasn't as central to Kentucky's economy as it had once been: by 2013, coal-mining employment had fallen to fewer than 17,000—a third the number of people employed in the state's far less storied auto-manufacturing sector, which had grown to the third-largest in the country. For another, coal mining in western Kentucky, part of the Illinois Basin, was holding on even as it declined in the east, suggesting that the challenge went beyond new regulations to the geological reality that Appalachian coal was getting more expensive to dig out.

McConnell's concern for the state's coal industry had long seemed directed more at the executives who supported his campaign than the workers themselves. In 2006, when yet another mine explosion claimed the lives of five miners in the Kentucky Darby LLC mine in Harlan County, an aide in McConnell's office spoke with Tony Oppegard, the former MSHA appointee who'd been kicked off the slurry spill investigation. Oppegard was representing some of the widows in the Darby Mine No. 1 disaster, and the aide urged the widows to call if they ever needed anything. Shortly afterward, they did need something: permission to sit in on meetings with MSHA. Oppegard called McConnell for assistance, and never heard back. "That was typical for us," he said. "When it came to an actual issue we needed help with, they didn't call back." Tom Buchanan, who led a group of small contractors in eastern Kentucky that do mine reclamation work, had a similar experience when they tried to set up meetings with McConnell in Washington to discuss the reclamation funding dedicated to the state. "He never did even meet with us," he says. "Oftentime we would call his office, and he never actually said no—he'd say we have an opening next Wednesday when he knew we were there this Wednesday."

It's not about being pro- or anti-coal, says Linc Chapman, back in Martin County. He is a staunch Republican and he himself worked in the mines, as a safety director. He accepts that when it comes to the side effects of coal mining, "you've got to have a certain amount of sacrifice to prosper." He just believes that the truly great disasters need to be avoided—and could be avoided if companies followed basic rules, and government held them to them. "If they did this right it would never have occurred," he says. "But when you've got the government in your pockets, you get by with what you want to get by with. Massey has a lot of political pull, and they let them slide. They didn't force them to do things right."

His fellow Inez resident, Mickey McCoy, puts it more bluntly: "Where was McConnell? Where was our representative? Where he's always been: in the back pocket of King Coal."

Chapter Three

FOLLOW THE LEADER

Bob Graham, the idiosyncratic Florida Democrat perhaps best remembered for keeping minutely detailed daily journals, joined the Senate in 1987, just two years after Mitch McConnell. Yet so much did McConnell keep to himself, and to his own party, that Graham had barely gotten to know his colleague from Kentucky—until, that is, they both had heart surgery within three days in early 2003 at Bethesda Naval Hospital.

McConnell had gone for a stress test recommended by the Capitol physician, and had failed it, leading to cardiac catheterization and instructions to undergo triple bypass surgery, pronto. Graham was there to have nonemergency surgery on his aortic heart valve. And in the week of convalescence that followed, they became postsurgical kindred spirits. Day after day, they walked up and down the hallways together to regain their strength. And they spent a lot of time talking, about, as Graham recalls it, "our families, what had brought us into politics, what we hoped to accomplish in politics."

Somewhat to his surprise, Graham liked his fellow patient. "I developed a very warm feeling toward Mitch," he says. "Mitch is by nature a little aloof—he doesn't have what some in politics have, that natural affinity and warmth for people. When I got to know him, I found him to be a more open and sympathetic and friendly person than under previous circumstances."

Yet that week away from the Sturm und Drang on Capitol Hill was not transformative in the broader sense. Both senators returned to a Senate more riven with every month. The upper chamber of the legislature had long prided itself on being less defined by partisan markers than the House of Representatives. The smaller size of the Senate gave it a clubby solidarity that the House lacked, its members served for longer terms and typically longer tenures than their counterparts in the House, giving them more time to get to know each other. They also represented entire states, encouraging a broadness of perspective that a House member representing a narrowly defined district might be less likely to have.

That singularity had been fading for some time, though. The parties had been sorting themselves out geographically and ideologically. One was far less likely than three decades prior to encounter a Northern liberal Republican senator or a conservative Southern Democrat. The increased cost of campaigning meant more time spent fund-raising and catering to party leaders or deep-pocketed funders who did not look so kindly on cross-aisle forays. Cable news had not helped matters. And the growing hegemony of the thirty-second ad as the ultimate campaign weapon had spurred senators to offer irrelevant amendments on bills to force the opposition to cast votes on hot-button issues that could be construed in unflattering ways in an eventual negative ad.

The evolution of the chamber could be traced in institutional increments, notably to the rise in the use of the filibuster—which in the past had been resorted to almost exclusively for the rare historic conflict, as on civil rights legislation—to stall or block routine legislation and nominations, to the point where it became necessary to have sixty votes to accomplish even the most rudimentary business. And it could be traced in episodes where the breakdown in comity was on display, from the judicial confirmation hearings for Robert Bork and Clarence Thomas to the ads run in 2002 against Georgia Democrat Max Cleland, a triple-amputee

Vietnam War veteran, by his Republican challenger, Saxby Chambliss, that linked Cleland to images of Osama bin Laden and declared Cleland did not have the "courage to lead" because he voted against Republicans on the structure of the new Department of Homeland Security. Chambliss won Cleland's seat, only heightening the partisan ill will in the chamber to which McConnell and Graham returned after their bipartisan recuperation in January 2003.

And it would get much worse. In 2007, after Democrats reclaimed majorities in both chambers in 2006 and Mitch McConnell ascended to become his party's leader in the Senate, the use of the filibuster soared—when Democrats were in the Senate minority during the Reagan years and George W. Bush years, there were, respectively, about 40 and 60 "cloture motions" to break or preempt filibusters filed per session, one commonly used measure of obstructionism. With the Republicans back in the minority in 2007 under McConnell's leadership, cloture motions spiked to 140 per session. By 2009, when the Democrats gained back the White House, the use of the filibuster spread, far more than ever before, to block presidential nominees of even the most pedestrian offices. "The idea of a filibuster as the expression of a minority that felt so intensely that it would pull out all the stops to block something pushed by the majority went by the boards," wrote Ornstein, the congressional scholar at the American Enterprise Institute, in 2014. "This was a pure tactic of obstruction, trying to use up as much of the Senate's most precious commodity—time—as possible to screw up the majority's agenda."

By 2011, the Senate and the rest of the gridlocked government found themselves on the brink of a national credit default, a brink reached again in another partisan standoff two years later, with the added bonus of a two-week-long shutdown of the federal government.

Bob Graham left the Senate in 2005, two years before McConnell took the helm of the Republican caucus. And from the vantage of southern Florida, Graham struggled to understand why the veteran senator whose company he had enjoyed in the hospital hallways had allowed Senate politics to come to this pass—in particular, why he had allowed the ideological wing of his caucus, a camp with so little regard for custom and comity that it often bordered on the gleefully nihilistic, to acquire such sway in Washington. Graham remembered other Republican leaders he had served alongside, and found it hard to believe they wouldn't have responded differently.

"I don't think that if the leader were of the ilk of a Bob Dole, if he had a sense of history and used history as a guide, that it would have happened like this," Graham says. "I don't know why they have fallen into what may bring short-term gains and maybe even some pleasure, but which maybe on a longer view of history is going to be very damning. . . . He is accommodating his hottest members, and they have not demonstrated any responsibility to the future or to how their actions are going to be seen in that long procession of time. I guess Mitch has made a decision that this wasn't a battle that he was going to take on."

———

The only thing Mitch McConnell wanted as much as winning elections for the Senate was winning elections within the Senate. Let other senators dream of running for president. For him, the dream was running the institution he had been revering since he was a boy. In this ambition, he was following the example of countless Southern politicians who had made the Senate their home in decades past, capitalizing on their own longevity in safe seats and the Senate's seniority system to dominate the institution well into the twentieth century. The Senate, wrote veteran *New York Times* congressional correspondent William S. White in the mid-1950s, was "peculiarly Southern both in flavor and structure," so much so that it had become, essentially, "the South's unending revenge . . . for Gettysburg." With its very Southern emphasis on courtliness and decorum—all those rules that "imposed a verbal impersonality on debate to ensure civility and formality," as LBJ biographer Robert Caro puts it—the Senate was the one political venue where McConnell's detached manner was not only not a hindrance, it was an asset. Here, formality conveyed authority, not discomfort.

Where other aspiring politicians steeped themselves in the legends of the White House, McConnell had immersed himself in the lore of the legislative branch's upper chamber. "He's a great student of the institution," says Dave Schiappa, who until 2013 served as McConnell's chief aide on the Senate floor. "He loves the history, loves to read everything he can get his hands on." This study wasn't just sentimental; it was geared toward learning the precedents and procedures that governed the chamber, a command that had helped McConnell's Southern forebears gain control over the institution. The lords of the Senate were his idols, and he wanted to be counted among them: "He's made a whole career of being the master of [the] Senate—the Republican version of LBJ, without the physical attributes," says Al Cross, a longtime political reporter with the *Courier-Journal* who now works at the University of Kentucky.

Partly, the drive to be majority leader was just a matter of ticking off the top item on the checklist. "There are things that he wants to accomplish in his career—while he's been majority whip, he's never been majority leader, and that's something he wants to have on his resume," says Lula Davis, a former chief aide to Harry Reid, the Democratic Senate leader. But one former Senate caucus leader notes that it goes deeper than that. Leadership in the chamber comes with its own kind of power high, one that seems to have held an especially strong allure for introverts like McConnell and his eventual counterpart, Reid. "The intensity, the extraordinary rush to be in those positions, it's addictive," the former caucus leader said. "It's the extraordinary exhilaration that comes with having these positions. . . . The intensity is almost like a drug."

McConnell had tried twice for the job of National Republican Senatorial Committee chairman, losing both times to Phil Gramm of Texas, before getting the post in 1997. As successful as he was at fund-raising and as much goodwill as he'd earned from his colleagues for leading the fight against campaign finance reform, his record at the helm of the campaign committee was mixed. In 1998, the Senate balance remained unchanged despite Democrats having to defend more seats, and in 2000 the Democrats gained a net total of four seats. In 2001, the Senate Republican caucus voted to replace him with Bill Frist, of Tennessee.

This setback did not dissuade McConnell from continuing his climb. He set about lining up votes for the next election for majority whip, the second-ranking spot in leadership. He had in his favor the gratitude for his stand against McCain-Feingold, and his performance in the 1995 sexual harassment investigation of fellow Republican Bob Packwood, of Oregon. In the role of Ethics Committee chairman, McConnell had come down hard on Packwood while taking the heat from Democrats for not making the investigation more transparent. Working against his ascension, though, was the fact that plenty of Republicans had not warmed to their tightly wound Kentucky colleague. Sure, there were occasional flashes of a dry, almost English sense of humor. That said, McConnell was, as his former chief of staff observed to the *Atlantic* in 2011, "the least personal politician I've ever been around."

But McConnell had a wingman. Bob Bennett, the towering senator from Utah who had stood almost alone with McConnell in opposing the anti-flag-burning amendment in 1995, would head out into the Republican caucus, one by one, feeling out senators about whether they might be inclined to support his friend over Larry Craig of Idaho, the other aspirant for the spot, who had not yet seen his career ended by a flirtatious encounter with an undercover male policeman in a bathroom at the Minneapolis airport. "He would go through every Republican in the

Senate and say, 'This one doesn't like me,' 'You go see this one, I've talked to him as far as I can go, if I push any further I'll push him over, you go see him,'" says Bennett. "He knew every single one of them."

The wingman would head out. "I would size up the opposition. Many times it was 'I really don't like Mitch that much, but I really don't like Larry.' You had to be careful—you can't be blatant about it. You go up and say, 'There's a leadership fight coming up, how do you feel between the two of them?' 'Well, you know, Mitch has his strengths,' and then you get them talking about Mitch's strengths. . . . Then I get the things he doesn't like about Mitch. Pretty soon I get the sense of how he feels about Mitch. I go back and say, 'He didn't like what you did here, you need to have a conversation about this, you need to do that.' So when Mitch would go see him, he was fore-armed with the intelligence I'd given him: 'Senator, you probably don't like what I did on such and such, I owe you an explanation on that.' So the door opened and Mitch would come back and say, 'Okay, we got him.'" When necessary, Bennett would try to undermine the opposition—subtly, of course. For instance, Bennett says, "John Warner [the former senator from Virginia] would say, 'It's far too early, I don't want to discuss it,' and I'd say, 'Okay, that's not a no,' and I'd keep at it: 'John, did you hear this [about Craig]?' and he'd say, 'I didn't like that.'" To which Bennett would respond, "'Well, there's always Mitch. . . .'"

McConnell and Bennett started this process with a year and a half to go before the vote would be held, a lesson McConnell told Bennett he had learned from Bob Livingston, the Louisiana congressman who had lined up all the support he needed to become House Speaker long before Newt Gingrich stepped down. "McConnell said, 'Livingston didn't get the speakership because he was the best candidate—he got it because he was the first.'" The early start paid off. By the time the summer of 2002 rolled around with the leadership elections looming later that year, McConnell sat down with Craig and presented him with a list of all the commitments he'd gotten. "Mitch was elected whip unanimously and Larry Craig decided he was going to do something else, because Mitch had it all lined up," Bennett says.

Soon afterward, McConnell and Bennett started using the same tactics to ready a run for the final rung, Republican leader— which at that point, in 2005, was also majority leader. They were well aware that Bill Frist had imposed a two-term limit on himself and would be gone after 2006—more aware than anyone else, says Bennett. "I don't think anyone else was thinking about what to do when Bill Frist leaves. Well, Mitch was thinking the first day Frist was chosen [as leader in 2002], what do we do when Frist leaves. We were talking about it. He knew exactly what he had to say to each senator, what he had to do to neutralize the ones opposed to him."

This calculus was rooted in McConnell's acute political instincts. Even if he wasn't close to that many of his colleagues, he knew where they were coming from, what they worried about, what they needed. "He knows what people are going to do long before they themselves see it," says Judd Gregg, the former Republican senator from New Hampshire. On Election Night in 2004, when Lincoln Chafee—whose father had stood with McConnell and Bennett in opposing the flag-burning amendment—saw George W. Bush holding on for a second term, it occurred to him that his reelection campaign in 2006 as a Republican in Rhode Island was going to be a whole lot tougher with Bush, who'd lost Chafee's state by 20 points, still in the White House.

The next day, McConnell called his liberal colleague to reassure him about his prospects two years hence—and to make sure he wasn't toying with switching parties, as his fellow liberal New Englander James Jeffords of Vermont had done three years earlier. "I was considering options—do I change parties, what do I do here, and he called me right away and said, 'Linc, I know what you're thinking. We want you to stay a Republican.' He was a mind reader that way. We all know you're going to have a rough race, and we'll get you the money we need.'" And they did. Asked by McConnell what sort of assistance he could use in Rhode Island, Chafee mentioned the hulking old bridge from the mainland to Jamestown, which the cash-strapped state had been meaning to take down for a dozen years. It cost $15 million. McConnell "immediately got it for me," and the bridge was detonated at last. There was a road project in Warwick that had run out of money, which required another $9 million. McConnell got that, too. It irked many in the party, going to such lengths for a Republican who had voted against Bush's tax cuts, the invasion of Iraq, and Supreme Court nominee Samuel Alito, and had even refused to support Bush's reelection in 2004. "There are many that would rather just purge the party, but he knew it was all about the math—he was going to need a Republican to keep the majority," Chafee says.

So determined was McConnell to hold the Senate majority in 2006, regardless of the cost, that in September of that year, with polls looking bleak for Republicans, he sought out Bush in a private meeting in the Oval Office to ask him to withdraw troops from Iraq to improve the party's chances in that fall's midterm election. Publicly, McConnell had been staunchly defending the war, but according to Bush, McConnell was so focused on the coming election cycle that he was willing to challenge Bush on the primary mission of his presidency. As Bush recounts in his memoir, McConnell told him, "Mr. President, your unpopularity is going to cost us control of the Congress." Bush said he responded: "Well, Mitch, what do you want me to do about it?" McConnell, in Bush's account, answered: "Mr. President, bring some troops home from Iraq." Bush's answer, as he recalls: "Mitch, I believe our presence in Iraq is necessary to protect America, and I will not withdraw troops unless military conditions warrant." He would, he told McConnell, "set troop levels to achieve victory in Iraq, not victory at the polls."

In the end, though, it was to no avail. Chafee lost his reelection, one of six incumbent Republican senators to lose that fall, giving the Democrats control of the chamber by a single vote. With his and Bennett's groundwork laid, McConnell would be elected Republican leader, but not majority leader.

And as diligent as his pursuit of his party's top spot had been, the effort required to attain it suggested that he would be able to rely less on sheer collegial affection to feel secure in his place than some of his predecessors had. It was a vulnerability that, if felt keenly enough, would have implications for managing the burgeoning right wing of his caucus, whose loyalties would come at a cost far greater than scattered millions for an old rusting bridge.

———————

There was a taut silence in the room that day in the summer of 2007 as the Senate Republican caucus absorbed what their leader had just said. Mitch McConnell had assembled the caucus behind closed doors to address a major setback, the passage of a sweeping ethics reform package with barely any input from Republicans. The Senate had passed an ethics bill that did contain plenty of points of agreement between McConnell and Harry Reid, the new majority leader, but that bill had never made it to a conference committee, where it could be melded with the version passed by the House. The reason? Jim DeMint, the first-term, hard-right Republican from South Carolina, had placed a hold on the appointment of conferees, claiming that he could not trust the committee not to water down provisions he had gotten into the Senate bill requiring much greater transparency for earmarks. So House Speaker Nancy Pelosi and Reid had figured out a way to pass a bill on their own, based primarily on the House version, and written to the liking of the Democrats.

Without naming DeMint, McConnell alluded to the hold and faulted it for leaving the Republicans in the lurch. It was an opaque allusion, but not so opaque that many members did not realize that McConnell had just called out DeMint in front of his colleagues. DeMint flared up and denied that he had forced the bad result, recalls Bob Bennett.

In a quiet but "very cold" voice, McConnell replied to the effect of: *Yes. Yes, you did.*

That's not fair, protested DeMint.

No, Jim. You're the one who did this, McConnell continued. *You're responsible for this outcome. . . . We did this to ourselves.*

There had never been anything like it. "It was the only time I have ever seen Mitch McConnell deal with a colleague in that kind of manner," Bennett says. "It was just a single sentence, but it left the whole room in stone-cold silence, because it was, 'All right, this is a rebuke that really matters.'"

The confrontation helped cement the rivalry between McConnell and the South Carolinian who had arrived in the Senate in 2005 burning to take on not only Democrats but Republicans complicit in deficit-widening travesties such as the Medicare drug benefit supported by McConnell and signed by President Bush. DeMint was at the helm of a small but vocal group of senators who interpreted their party's loss of the Senate as punishment for the party's drift from budget-cutting orthodoxy. They had little patience for institutional niceties, among them deference to leadership.

What was most notable about the confrontation, though, was what Bennett stressed in recounting it—its singularity. McConnell was willing to give DeMint opaque reprimands behind closed doors on matters of institutional prerogative—senators' right to award earmarks, or relying on seniority in making assignments to the influential Appropriations Committee, another issue where McConnell resisted DeMint. ("Jim, you can't change the Senate," he chided, according to DeMint.)

But when it came to the big issues, what McConnell would project to the public was the spectacle of a leader submitting to the gravitational pull of DeMint and the wing of the party he represented. Back home in Kentucky after the 2006 election, McConnell had predicted a productive session ahead of a meeting of the Farm Bureau. "Gridlock is not my first choice," he said. "My first choice is to accomplish things for the country. You all didn't send us up there just to play games and engage in sparring rounds." To his national audience, though, McConnell was sounding a more defiant tone, as if already seeking to mollify the DeMints within his caucus. "It takes sixty votes to do just about everything in the Senate. Forty-nine is a robust minority," he told the conservative radio host Hugh Hewitt. "Nothing will leave the Senate that doesn't have our imprint. We'll either stop it if we think it's bad for America, or shape it, hopefully right of center."

Of course, it takes sixty votes to do just about everything only if the minority opts to use the power of the filibuster for, well, just about everything. And McConnell held true to his promise to Hewitt to do just that. He led his caucus to block Democratic efforts to raise the minimum wage from $5.15 to $7.25, forcing them to add business tax breaks to the bill. They blocked Democratic legislation to start drawing down troops in Iraq. They blocked bills to make it easier for unions to organize workers, to provide in-state tuition at public universities for undocumented students, to close the detention center at Guantanamo Bay. In 2008, McConnell forced Senate clerks to read the entirety of a 492-page Democratic bill to reduce greenhouse gas emissions, a process that took ten hours. Harry Reid linked this tactic to a Republican memo, given him by a lobbyist, that outlined the Republican plan to delay the bill before killing it to stoke voter upset at the Democrats about high energy prices. "You couldn't make anything up more cynical," Reid said on the Senate floor.

McConnell's prominence in leading the opposition to all these measures made it all the more conspicuous when, on the legislation most important to President Bush, he vanished. Back in 2006, McConnell had supported the comprehensive reform of the nation's immigration system that Bush had been seeking as part of his effort to salvage some "compassionate conservatism" and build his party's appeal among Latino voters. Now, in 2007, Bush was making another try, this time with Harry Reid and John McCain as bipartisan allies. McConnell pronounced the bill an improvement over the 2006 version, but implacable immigration opponents, led by DeMint, did not agree, decrying the bill's "amnesty" for illegal aliens. When the bill came to the floor the crucial vote to open consideration of the legislation, McConnell's second and third in command, Jon Kyl of Arizona and Trent Lott of Mississippi, both from states with strong anti-immigrant sentiment, voted to allow consideration. So did Lindsey Graham, who was facing reelection the year following in DeMint's home state, South Carolina.

McConnell waited until enough votes had been cast to make it clear that the bill was going to fall short of the necessary sixty, and then voted against it as well. In an unusual withdrawal, the Republican leader did not even speak on the floor until after the bill's fate was known. He was, *Roll Call* reported, "a virtual no-show." Conservative columnist Robert Novak went further, calling it a "truly major failure of leadership." McConnell might have been willing to stand up to DeMint in private on a matter of importance to congressional insiders, but here, on an issue of far greater visibility and with his own reelection looming, he buckled to the wave DeMint and his camp had generated.

The stakes were even higher a year later, in 2008, when McConnell faced off against DeMint yet again. World financial markets were in free fall and Bush's Treasury secretary, Hank Paulson, readied a massive, $700 billion bailout for the banks to cushion the collapse. Once again, DeMint rallied opposition. His conservative counterparts in the House blocked the package, sending the Dow Jones Industrial Average plunging by 778 points. This market gyration helped drive home the gravity of the situation, and the rescue would pass on a second try. Over in the Senate, McConnell opted to stand against DeMint. But his willingness to act responsibly and get the package passed was grudging. Democratic staff knowledgeable about the negotiations say that McConnell's contribution to the talks was, essentially, "How many votes do you really need?"—the implication being that, even with a Republican president making the request for the rescue and with crisis looming, he did not want to make any more members of his caucus go along with it than necessary. A third of Senate Republicans voted against the rescue.

Still, it seemed conceivable that with the immediate crisis past, McConnell may have reassessed his accommodating position toward the DeMint wing. Their recklessness had come close to exacerbating the biggest global financial emergency in decades. McConnell had survived his reelection and wouldn't face voters again for another six years. And his party had just suffered its second consecutive thumping at the polls, leaving it without control of either the White House or Congress and underscoring the need for a period of rebuilding and self-examination.

A sign that he might be inclined to embrace such sobriety came with his Christmastime request to Richard Lugar, his veteran colleague from Indiana, now considered among the more moderate members of the caucus. He hoped Lugar would officially renominate him as caucus leader. "I got the call out in Indianapolis. He anticipated a challenge, and he was hopeful I would give a rousing speech nominating him for the new caucus—which I was delighted to do," Lugar recalls. "He sensed that those forces were closing in on him, not to mention the rest of the party . . . and he thought I had the respect of the colleagues, that if I really took the thing in hand . . . that I was going to settle it." And indeed, while there were "murmurs of some potential difficulties," Lugar says, "after I spoke and someone called for a vote, he was unanimously elected."

The retention of his leadership post, helped by one of the party's old guard, might have led to a broader resolve on McConnell's part to take on those "forces closing in" on his party.

Quite the opposite.

———

Jeff Merkley had known Congress when it functioned. He had been a Senate intern in the 1970s and worked as a congressional aide and a staffer for the Congressional Budget Office in the 1980s, which had left him with a "love for institution, a respect for it." "I knew that senators may have carried different party labels, but they generally liked each other and generally wanted to work together. They realized that for twenty percent [of the issues], that's what campaigns were about, but they could get a lot done addressing the other issues. What was particularly different was that there wasn't an effort to just immobilize the Senate."

Now, in early 2009, as a newly elected Democratic senator from Oregon, Merkley often had the rookie's inglorious task of serving as the presiding officer who must watch over the chamber for hours on end while senators hold forth to a chamber empty but for tourists and pages refilling water glasses. And for much of that time in 2009, it seemed, the person whom Merkley found himself listening to was Mitch McConnell. Day after day, "he would just reel off the most partisan talking points possible, with no indication of advocacy or working together to solve the most pressing problems of the country," Merkley said. Listening to McConnell, he says, "crystallized" what had gone wrong in the Senate since he'd been there as a young man. "It's just a tremendous problem for America to have a perpetual partisan campaign, the inability to say, 'The elections are over, let's work together to solve some of these big issues.'"

That was not the path McConnell had chosen. In the midwinter of 2009, as Barack Obama assumed the presidency and the country was losing six hundred thousand jobs per month, McConnell assembled his caucus for a retreat in West Virginia and laid out a strategy that focused a whole lot more on undermining the former than addressing the latter. As Bennett recalls, "Mitch said, 'We have a new president with an approval rating in the seventy percent area. We do not take him on frontally. We find issues where we can win, and we begin to take him down, one issue at a time. We create an inventory of losses, so it's Obama lost on this, Obama lost on that. And we wait for the time where the image has been damaged to the point where we can take him on. We recognize the American people—even those who do not approve of him—want him to have success, are hopeful.'" In other words: wait out Americans' hopefulness in a dire moment for the country until it curdles to disillusionment.

This strategy meant discouraging the sort of cross-partisan goodwill that Obama had held out as one of the central promises of his presidency, and that seemed within reach amid the celebratory feelings around his historic inauguration. So when New Hampshire senator Judd Gregg, who had served as a sort of untitled consigliere to McConnell, informed him that he was considering Obama's invitation to become his secretary of commerce, McConnell did not congratulate him. "I went and told him and he understood I was going to do it, but he clearly thought it was a bad idea," Gregg says. "It was obvious from his body language that he thought it was a bad idea." Shortly afterward, Gregg withdrew his nomination, citing "irresolvable conflicts" with Obama.

The strategy meant seeking leverage, at a time when diminished Republican ranks would seem to offer little of it, by bogging down the machinery of government on even the most mundane matters. In the first weeks of 2009, a big omnibus bill to expand wilderness protection that had been cobbled together for months, with provisions to please just about every senator and state, was held up for days as Tom Coburn, of Oklahoma protested the measure. A few weeks later, Coburn was at the center of the attempted delay of another measure with broad support, a bill to reform the credit card industry—he managed to attach an unrelated amendment lifting the ban on loaded firearms in national parks, forcing Democrats to choose between accepting a pet issue of the National Rifle Association and postponement of reforms of an industry that had figured in the nation's consumer debt crisis. Most vulnerable to delays were the administration's nominations—Republicans mounted filibusters against obscure figures such as a deputy secretary for the Interior Department and counsel to the Commerce Department. By year's end, seventy-five nominees were still hung up in the Senate.

The strategy meant seizing on the first signs of weakness—"issues where we can win," as McConnell had put it—which is what Republicans did after Obama ordered, on his first day in office, the closure within one year of the detention facility at Guantanamo Bay. Fomenting controversy around that issue was McConnell's brainchild, says his friend Bob Bennett. "He came to us and said, 'I've found the issue where he's going to lose: Guantanamo. We're going to oppose the closing of Guantanamo. There's a majority out there that do not want Guantanamo closed. We can talk about taking terrorists and putting them on American soil and terrorists causing prison riots and things of that kind.'" Senate Republicans spent a lot of time talking about that, and by the time the administration proposed in late 2009 moving some detainees to a federal prison in Illinois, the public was primed for a backlash. Guantanamo remained open and became a glaring emblem of Obama's unfulfilled promise. "It was the beginning of, 'Maybe this guy doesn't walk on water,'" says Bennett.

Above all, though, the strategy meant holding the Republican caucus together to deny Obama Republican votes on his highest-priority initiatives. The Republicans would not follow the lead of the Democrats who, in the early years of George W. Bush's administration, had voted for his two rounds of tax cuts and the Iraq war resolution. Instead, they would form a cohesive opposition force, regardless of the inducements thrown their way. Achieving such unity was, on one level, not difficult to achieve—life in the minority lends itself to solidarity. "In the minority it's easier to maintain control of your caucus," says Lula Davis, the former chief aide to Harry Reid. "If you don't stay together, you don't have a chance in hell of getting anything done." Still, it was hard to imagine someone better suited to keeping members in line than Mitch McConnell. He had his fund-raising largesse. He had a top-notch staff to keep on top of things. And he had the political astuteness gained from years in the Senate—and years prior studying it—to know what he needed to do to keep members from straying when it mattered. "He's a good listener and can read his members very well," says Davis. "It was fascinating, watching him shepherd them and keep them together all the time. . . . He understands every issue to the nth degree."

There were, of course, weapons at a leader's disposal—committee assignments, campaign cash, and the like—but rarely did McConnell apply them in the blunt fashion of Lyndon Johnson. The pressure was more modulated than that, says Bennett. "He very, very seldom lowers the leadership hammer, very seldom said, 'I'm the leader and I want your support in this, you've got to be with me.' But when he does, he's very, very firm, and makes it extremely difficult for you to say no, because he doesn't do it in a routine fashion, so that when he does do it, you know this is really serious and important and if I disappoint Mitch this time, he's going to remember."

At times, Bennett says, he'd gone to McConnell and said, "Look, I can't be with you because of stuff at home, or this is a really dumb idea and my conscience won't let me," to which McConnell would respond, "That's okay, Bob." But that allowance comes with a cost: "He lets you off the hook enough times so that when he comes to you and says, 'I need you,' you have to," says Bennett. "He'll say, 'Bob, you're my best friend in the caucus and everyone knows it—if you don't come with me on this one . . .' How do you say no?" So implicit was the pressure that its traces often weren't immediately discernible after the fact, Bennett says. "I have never seen him say, 'If you do this, I'll see to that.' But some people will say, 'How did [this or that senator] get on [the

Finance Committee]? Why did Mitch do this or that? I can't understand,' . . . and I'll say, 'Wait a minute, look back at this [vote],
and this, and this,' and they'll say, 'Ah, okay.'"

On the first big Senate vote of Obama's presidency, the unit
held—almost. The White House and congressional Democrats
had filled the economic recovery package with $288 billion in tax
cuts, more than they wanted and more than many economists
thought useful for effective stimulus, in an effort to win Republican backing. The inducements managed to win zero House
Republicans and only three in the Senate—far short of the consensus Obama wanted for his big measure to address the economic collapse, but just enough to get the bill passed and enough
to allow Democrats to claim, in a bit of a stretch, that the bill was
"bipartisan."

Mitch McConnell would make sure that did not happen again.

———

Max Baucus, the senior senator from Montana and the chairman
of the Senate Finance Committee, had a list. From the start of the
Obama administration, Baucus had taken it upon himself to lay the
groundwork for one of the new president's top priorities, achieving
near universal health coverage in a country where some 50 million
lacked insurance. Baucus developed a white paper sketching out a
legislative framework, and a long list of Republican senators who
he thought might support the bill.

Why bother with the list? After all, by the time Pennsylvania's
Arlen Specter switched parties in late April from Republican to
Democrat, the Democrats had enough votes in the Senate to break
a filibuster. But Baucus knew how much Obama spoke about transcending partisan divides—and he knew how important it was to
get bipartisan backing for major changes in social policy. Implementation and national acceptance would be hard without some
measure of consensus. After all, Social Security and Medicare had
both gotten more than a dozen Republican votes in the Senate.

Even in the more polarized twenty-first century, the Medicare drug benefit had passed in 2003 with a dozen Democratic votes—including Baucus's.

Baucus had reason to believe he might get some Republican support. After all, the framework he was drawing up was modeled on proposals that had been offered by the conservative Heritage Foundation and by Republicans seeking an alternative to Hillary Clinton's health-care plan in 1993. Governor Mitt Romney, a Republican, had signed similar legislation into law in Massachusetts. Baucus's approach did not seek to replace private insurers with government-run, "single-payer" insurance like Medicare, but rather sought to cover the uninsured via private insurance, with subsidies and a mandate requiring individuals to get coverage to make the system work.

And at first, Baucus was getting encouraging responses. No small number of Republicans told him they might just be able to sign on to his plan, particularly if he left out the "public option," a government-run insurance plan to be offered alongside private plans.

As the spring of 2009 wore on and as the debate began in earnest on Baucus's committee and several others in both chambers, the Republicans who'd earlier expressed interest started falling away. By summer, Baucus was left communicating with three Republicans—Mike Enzi of Wyoming, Olympia Snowe of Maine, and Chuck Grassley of Iowa. Enzi was the most conservative of the three and Snowe the most moderate, but Grassley, the top Republican on the Finance Committee, was the one Baucus was most counting on to bring a substantial minority of Republicans onto the bill. The debonair Baucus and the ornery Grassley had, even in these partisan times, worked together on major legislation that came through their committee—including on the Medicare drug benefit and George W. Bush's tax cuts, all of which Baucus had supported, to the dismay of many of his Democratic colleagues. And Baucus had filled his draft with items he knew

Grassley favored, such as a requirement that drug and device makers disclose financial relationships with doctors and hospitals, and rewards to hospitals that provide high-quality care under Medicare.

But if Grassley was tempted by these inducements and any feeling of obligation to Baucus for the Democrat's support of Bush's big initiatives, he was also getting persuasive warnings to resist them—not from DeMint or other archconservatives in the caucus, but from its leader. McConnell, Grassley says, made it clear that he found the legislation misguided, whatever its ideological origins. "Mitch had his mind well made up that this sort of approach that could lead to the nationalization of health care wasn't right and wasn't good for the country and might happen as a result of those meetings" with Baucus, says Grassley.

McConnell did not outright order Grassley and the two other Republicans against participating in the discussions. Rather, Grassley says, he told them, "I just think you ought to be cautious." As effective was the persistent message the three Republicans were getting at caucus meetings held every Wednesday at 4 P.M. at a big square table in the Mansfield Room in the Capitol to discuss the health-care legislation. Grassley would update his fellow Republicans on what was going on in the talks with Baucus and the two other Democrats in the "Gang of Six" (Jeff Bingaman of New Mexico and Kent Conrad of North Dakota). The reaction he encountered every week made it clear that it was going to be very difficult to bring a critical mass of Republicans around. "Those regular meetings led people around to the point [of thinking] that this isn't something as good as when we first started talking about it," says Grassley. "I'm not sure if [McConnell] led them there but he put in place a process that brought around the consensus that Obamacare wasn't good."

Others at the meetings say it was plain that Grassley's heart wasn't in going up against McConnell and the prevailing sentiment, so grudging were his attempts to sell the Gang of Six's work to the caucus. "Grassley never committed to anything" with Baucus, says Bob Bennett. "It was 'I'll take that back and see if that would fly' and it never would—all of the stuff he brought back to us, including some of the stuff he felt might work, he never came back and advocated for it." And once Grassley started hearing from his Iowa constituents attacking the legislation at town hall meetings in August, he turned critical of the legislation, telling three hundred Iowans at one event that they had "every right to fear" that the bill's provision of Medicare coverage for end-of-life-counseling—a provision he had recently championed—could turn into a "government program that determines if you're going to pull the plug on grandma." For the Democrats in the Gang of Six, this distancing was confounding, because there was no concrete point of disagreement to negotiate over. "I didn't identify any specific policy issue where if we'd agreed to make a change in that aspect of the bill," agreement would be reached, says Bingaman. "I didn't detect that. They just became less and less willing to sign on to the bill as we got further and further into the discussions."

Grassley's turn against his former positions and Baucus prompted speculation on the Hill about what McConnell might have offered or threatened to effect the switch—say, the loss of Grassley's top spot on the Finance Committee. Grassley dismisses the committee rumor, but in doing so lends some credence to another version of the speculation, that McConnell had made clear to him that if he went along with Baucus, he'd face a primary challenge from the right in 2012—and would not get help from his party in fending it off. "There was no threat [over committee rank], never a discussion like that," Grassley says. "Probably more of a concern would've been in the state of Iowa, whether I would have had Tea Party opposition."

Snowe was facing a similar prospect—if anything, more so than Grassley. Every few days, it seemed, another busload of conservative activists would come down from Maine to confront her. And just as often, a member of the Senate Republican leadership of their staff would demand to know: was she switching parties? Senate Republicans deny that she was coming under collegial censure for her negotiations with Baucus—"You never knew where Olympia was going to end up on something like this," says Judd Gregg. "No one tried to influence Olympia." Still, she, like Grassley, had reason to fear she could not depend on McConnell and the rest of the party to back her up if she broke from them on the legislation and faced a primary challenge as a result. Snowe voted for the legislation in the Finance Committee, but when it reached the Senate floor two months later, she joined every other Republican in voting against it. Her vote against the bill was so conflicted to the end that, as one observer of the roll call noted, she could barely get out her "no"—it sounded more like "*nyeo.*"

The legislation did not pass into law until the following March, after being postponed and nearly derailed by the election of a Republican to fill Kennedy's seat in Massachusetts. So tortured and drawn-out had the process been that, historic as the law was, its public reception was cool. And credit for this reception, Senate Republicans say, went to McConnell. Rather than trying to block the bipartisan negotiations from the outset, he had let them proceed, knowing that they were unlikely to bear fruit (especially if subtle pressure was applied throughout to the participants) and that the longer they went on, the more unpopular the legislation would become with a public that has little patience for endless haggling. "He said, 'Our strategy is to delay this sucker as long as we possibly can, and the longer we delay it the worse the president looks: why can't he get it done? He's got sixty votes? We're gonna delay it, delay it, and delay it as long we can,'" says Bennett. "Every time something would come up, he would find a way to delay it."

When the senators headed out for that 2009 summer recess, Bennett says, McConnell told his members "your goal is to have

Congress come back more hesitant about Obamacare than they were at the end of July." And indeed, when Bennett spoke with Ron Wyden, the Oregon Democrat, after the break, Wyden told Bennett, "You Republicans won August—this turkey is a whole lot less popular now." After which, Bennett says, "we dragged that sucker out until December." He concludes: "You look back on it and that's a virtuoso performance when you only have forty votes. That's why Mitch was encouraging the Gang of Six—that was a way to delay this. He was on top of the whole thing."

———

One day in the first half of 2009, as the health-care debate was heating up, McConnell approached Chris Dodd in the Senate and told the Connecticut Democrat what Max Baucus would learn months later: "I can't think of a formulation for health care we're going to be able to support." As Dodd recalls, McConnell went on to say: "With financial reform there is, there's space there" for agreement.

So, Dodd made far less effort than Baucus would to get Republican backing for the portions of the health-care bill moving through the Health, Education, Labor and Pensions Committee, which Dodd chaired. But when it came time to take up the big financial reform bill, Dodd was confident he could engineer the sort of consensus that the health-care legislation had been denied. "I was determined to demonstrate how the Senate could work," he says. After all, this bill wasn't legislation to expand the safety net at a cost to wealthy Americans, but to fix a financial system so out of whack that the American economy had entered its biggest slump since the Great Depression. Dodd worked closely for weeks with Bob Corker, the Tennessee Republican, hoping that the former construction and real estate magnate could bring a whole swath of his caucus onto the bill. He included plenty of provisions that Corker wanted in the draft, including limits on the new Consumer Financial Protection Bureau.

But just as Baucus had found with Grassley on health care, Corker began to back away. Dodd was pretty sure he knew what was up: that McConnell had told Corker, "Don't you dare negotiate with Dodd." In the end, Dodd managed to get four Republicans: the three New Englanders and, ironically enough, Chuck Grassley. Once again Obama was denied a big, truly bipartisan achievement, and the bill became more partisan fodder. As it moved through Congress, pollster Frank Luntz was coaching Republicans to cast it as a "bailout for the banks"—never mind that Wall Street lobbyists were fighting it every step of the way.

Another seeming opportunity for a consensus arose earlier in 2010—a proposal by the top Democrat and Republican on the Senate Budget Committee—Conrad and Gregg—to establish an eighteen-member bipartisan commission to come up with recommendations to reduce the federal deficit that would be "fast-tracked" through Congress. The bill had nineteen Republican cosponsors—and the seeming support of Mitch McConnell. On the Senate floor in May 2009, McConnell had said, "We must address the issue of entitlement spending now before it is too late. As I have said many times before, the best way to address the crisis is the Conrad-Gregg proposal, which would provide an expedited pathway for fixing these profound long-term challenges. . . . So I urge the administration, once again, to support the Conrad-Gregg proposal."

The administration did just that. Shortly before the bill was to come up in the Senate, Obama came out in favor of it, to the consternation of many liberals who thought the administration should still be pushing for more stimulus for the listing economy, rather than austerity measures. But on January 26, 2010, the bill fell short of a filibuster-proof majority, 53–46. McConnell voted against it—as did seven of the Republicans who originally cosponsored it. McConnell's shift on the bill drew a harsh condemnation from, among others, Fred Hiatt, the deficit-hawk editor of the *Washington Post* editorial page:

No single vote by any single senator could possibly illustrate everything that is wrong with Washington today. No single vote could embody the full cynicism and cowardice of our political elite at its worst, or explain by itself why problems do not get solved. But here's one that comes close. . . . It's impossible to avoid the conclusion that the only thing that changed since May is the political usefulness of the proposal to McConnell's partisan goals. He was happy to claim fiscal responsibility while beating up Obama for fiscal recklessness. But when Obama endorsed the idea, as he did on the Saturday before the vote—and when the commission actually, against all odds, had the wisp of a chance of winning the needed 60 Senate votes—McConnell bailed.

Gregg, who left the Senate at the end of 2010, says he never found out from McConnell why he had turned on the proposal. "I never asked that question. I accepted the fact some of us didn't like the idea and didn't vote for it," he says. "At one point he thought it was a good idea but he didn't vote for it. . . . I didn't follow up on it—there was no point in asking."

Conrad, who retired two years later, is more open about the disappointment. "None of those guys ever talked to me about it," he says. "But to lose when seven of your original cosponsors vote against it, that was a surprise, that's for sure. . . . We didn't know if we'd prevail, but we knew if the seven cosponsors had voted for it, we would have."

In the months that followed, McConnell offered a reply of sorts to Conrad, Hiatt, and others bothered by that vote. In a candid comment to the *New York Times* in March 2010, McConnell explained why he had worked so hard to withhold Republican support on big issues like health care: "It was absolutely critical that everybody be together because if the proponents of the bill were able to say it was bipartisan, it tended to convey to the public this this is okay, they must have figured it out."

He elaborated on this to an *Atlantic* reporter, later in 2010: "We worked very hard to keep our fingerprints off of these proposals because we thought—correctly, I think—that the only way the American people would know that a great debate was going on was if the measures were not bipartisan. When you hang the 'bipartisan' tag on something, the perception is that differences have been worked out, and there's a broad agreement that that's the way forward."

It was a revealing window into McConnell's thinking: in an institution that had prided itself so much on bipartisan comity—that had evolved to *require* bipartisan comity, thanks to the expanding use of the filibuster and other procedural customs—here the Republican leader stated that he had done his utmost to deny bipartisan support to the president's initiatives as a matter of policy, across the board. The strategy was devious and brilliant. McConnell knew how much voters hated partisan strife, that it soured them on government in general, and that this souring would hurt the party in power—particularly if the party in power was also the party that advocated for more government. He knew that the public tended to tune out the details of partisan haggling, and that his party would therefore be unlikely to suffer for blatant reversals such as the flip on the deficit commission. He knew that he not only had Fox News and the rest of the conservative media on his side, but that the mainstream press would be reluctant to enlighten the public about who was at fault for gridlock—many commentators were loath to get into policy particulars, and even more loath to be seen as favoring one side over the other. McConnell, while no media darling like his rival John McCain, had been adept at stoking the perception of liberal bias in the media, thus making image-conscious reporters wary of describing dysfunction fully. Again and again, reports on bills blocked by GOP filibusters would refer to Democrats' failure to pass a bill, without noting that it had received a majority of votes in the Senate—just not the sixty to break a Republican filibuster.

And McConnell knew how much Obama had staked on the promise of transcending partisan divides in Washington, and that denying him the opportunity to do so would come to seem like a defining failure of his presidency.

This strategy came at a cost to McConnell's party—on major issues of the day, legislation that would shape whole swaths of American life and business for years to come, Republicans had ceded influence over the final product. So desperate were Baucus, Dodd, and Obama for bipartisan credibility that serious concessions were well within reach. "I don't think there's anything [Obama] wouldn't have given away to get a couple Republicans," says Dennis Kelleher, a former top Democratic Senate leadership aide. One of the Republican staffers who worked on the bill says Grassley and others should have made the most of that leverage: "The way it's always worked is, if you see the other side is going to win, you're going, let's sit down and get some stuff your way." Several conservative commentators noted this lost opportunity after the health-care legislation passed. "We went for all the marbles [and] we ended with none," wrote former George W. Bush speechwriter David Frum.

And several Democrats expressed bemused gratitude that Republicans had allowed them to shape both the health-care and financial reform bills as they saw fit. Yes, the Democrats would suffer at the polls in 2010, but they had also managed to pass transformative legislation when they had the opportunity to do so. "No question, McConnell basically told them, 'No cooperation,'" says Barney Frank, the since-retired Massachusetts Democrat who led the financial reform push in the House. "But heck, he did us a favor! Chris [Dodd] was hoping for a seventy-five-vote bill. Well, a seventy-five-vote bill would have been weaker. McConnell gave us the freedom of 'nothing left to lose.'"

But the opportunity for his party to shape legislation on big issues was, for McConnell, secondary to the overriding goal, which he laid out in another interview, one month before the 2010 midterm elections. A *National Journal* reporter asked McConnell what his party would tell voters if it won back Congress that fall.

"We need to be honest with the public," he replied. "This election is about them, not us. And we need to treat this election as the first step in retaking the government. We need to say to everyone on Election Day, 'Those of you who helped make this a good day, you need to go out and help us finish the job.'"

"What's the job?" the reporter asked.

"The single most important thing we want to achieve," McConnell answered, "is for President Obama to be a one-term president."

It was, without a doubt, the most-quoted remark Mitch McConnell had ever uttered. In fewer than twenty words, he had managed to crystallize his strategy of obstructing and undermining Obama above all else. To Kelleher, the former Senate Democratic leadership aide, the quote confirmed what he had observed since the start of 2009—that McConnell seemed to harbor a deep contempt for the new president. "The Obama election reinvigorated Mitch McConnell and gave him a reason for being," says Kelleher. "He genuinely dislikes him . . . and thinks the guy has no business being in the White House." Here, after all, was a president who'd arrived in the Senate only four years earlier from the Illinois state legislature and barely been able to conceal his bored disdain for the institution that defined McConnell's entire existence. McConnell and his Republican colleagues "all thought he was a lightweight—'there's a guy who can give a speech, big fucking deal,'" says Kelleher. "Obama is the ultimate kind of outsider, and outsiders who don't adhere to the [institutional] mores are never liked."

But there was another explanation for McConnell's bald declaration of his supreme motivation. Quite simply, it sprang from the mind-set that had been governing McConnell since his arrival in

Washington more than a quarter century earlier: What mattered above all else was that you and your party prevailed in the next election cycle. "You are only as good as the next election," McConnell liked to say. And: "You have to be elected before you can be a statesman." Seen in this light, McConnell was not expressing some special animus against Barack Obama; he was giving a clear insight into his political philosophy.

First, though, there was the matter of winning the most immediate cycle, the 2010 midterm election, and with it, perhaps, the Senate majority and thus the majority leader job McConnell had thought he was going to assume four years earlier. The party's prospects were looking good, with its base voters energized by their anti-Obama fury, his big spending and his "overreach" on health care. Conservative Republicans were so furious, in fact, that one of their first elective acts was to jettison from the party's ticket in Utah McConnell's closest ally in the Senate, Bob Bennett. At the state's GOP convention, an archconservative lawyer replaced him.

Bennett's defeat was a blow to McConnell. He had lost a confidant, and Bennett had been targeted precisely because he was a member in good standing of the Republican establishment in Washington. Like McConnell, he had voted for the financial bailout in 2008. But it was not hard to see the defeat another way, too—that McConnell himself had helped fuel the Tea Party insurgency that had toppled his friend. It was McConnell's strategy to withhold any Republican participation in Obama's top legislative initiatives, which had guaranteed that Obama and the Democrats would appear to be pushing through their agenda with brute partisan force. It was McConnell's decision to torpedo the proposed debt commission in 2010, which had guaranteed that no grand effort would be undertaken to narrow the deficit, one of the Tea Partiers' main fixations. And it was his persistent drumbeat against the *"far left"* Obama that helped fire up the grass roots. If even the sedate Mitch McConnell was so outraged by Obama, the situation must be really bad—but why weren't McConnell and his establishment allies *doing* more to stop him?

Bennett, for one, declines to speculate whether the insurgency that ended his Senate career would have been less out of control had McConnell approached the role of opposition differently. "I would be very loath to challenge his motives or his decisions," he says. "Mitch had to make a decision as to what would work and what wouldn't, what would preserve his power over the long term and what he had to concede over the short term to do that. I can't second-guess his decision about what he did."

McConnell was reckoning with the insurgency closer to home, as well. There, he had pressured the increasingly unpredictable Bunning, his fellow Republican senator from Kentucky, to retire and had selected secretary of state Trey Grayson, a mild-mannered Harvard graduate, to replace him. A libertarian ophthalmologist from Bowling Green had another idea. Rand Paul came into the race with a profile that tested the bounds of acceptability—he opposed key elements of the Civil Rights Act, for instance—but by tapping into the same vein of outrage as had Bennett's challenger in Utah, he pulled even with Grayson—and then ahead of him. Implicit in Paul's challenge of Grayson was his challenge of McConnell, who had for some time now called the shots on who ran for what in the Kentucky GOP. And on the weekend of the Kentucky Derby, with two weeks remaining before the May primary, McConnell decided to make his support for Grayson explicit, even if it meant violating general party protocol. Grayson's campaign aired, in heavy statewide rotation and with "everything we had behind it," says Grayson, an ad with McConnell declaring: "I rarely endorse in primaries, but these are critical times. I know Trey Grayson and trust him. We need Trey's conservative leadership to help turn back the Obama agenda."

When the ad went up, Grayson's internal polling showed him within reach of Paul. Two weeks later, Paul won by 20 percentage points—a shift that Grayson now views as not unrelated to the ad, which he says failed to account for the anti-establishment fervor on the right. "We all thought it was going to put me over the top," says Grayson. "We were wrong."

On primary night, McConnell called Grayson from Washington. But it wasn't to commiserate about the failure of McConnell's whole plan to elevate Grayson. It was to make sure that Grayson knew he needed to get on board with Rand Paul, quickly and convincingly. "Mitch encouraged me . . . be a good loser, endorse the candidate, and don't delay," Grayson says. "He was encouraging me, do the right things that are the hard things. . . . You have to do this, not for yourself, but for the party. It's gonna be hard, but it's the right thing to do." Grayson did as he was told and went to the state capital, Frankfort, and party headquarters—which are named for McConnell—for a "unity rally" a few days later. His deed done, he wandered out of the building while, inside, Mitch McConnell and Rand Paul, two people who barely knew each other, began the task of building one of the stranger alliances American politics has ever seen. The speed with which McConnell had embraced Paul perhaps should not have come as a surprise. In his memoir *The Great American Awakening,* Jim DeMint describes the meeting in which he told McConnell that he would be supporting Paul over Grayson. He expected McConnell to be angry, but found instead that McConnell was relieved to hear that DeMint's endorsement of Paul would make clear that he still supported McConnell as leader. "After that a lot of the tension in the room evaporated," DeMint writes. As much as McConnell preferred Grayson over Paul, his priority above all was that the insurgents in his state did not turn against him, too.

There was more of the fallout to come. In September, Alaska senator Lisa Murkowski lost her state's Republican primary to a highly conservative challenger. Instead of stepping aside, Murkowski opted to stay on the November ballot—as a write-in independent candidate. This decision brought the party's civil war to the doorstep of the Republican Senate caucus, in the form of a concrete question: what to do with a Republican member now running against someone who had won the party's primary? Murkowski resigned her caucus leadership position, but there remained the question of whether to strip her of her rank as the top Republican on the Energy and Natural Resources Committee, a crucial slot for a senator from Alaska who relied on the support of energy industry lobbyists. There was a "big fight" within the conference, says Bob Bennett, with DeMint leading the charge to punish Murkowski. McConnell initially suggested that Murkowski be replaced with an acting ranking member on the energy committee, but after a debate, the conference voted—in secret ballot, with the tally undisclosed even to the conference—in favor of keeping Murkowski in the top spot. McConnell instructed members not to discuss the fight beyond a one-line public statement: "Lisa has stepped down from her position on [the NRSC] and we took no further action."

This result did not sit well with DeMint, who, Bennett recalls, "gets on the Internet and puts out an email denouncing all of us and screams and yells and tries to create fund-raising for Miller." ("The good ol' boys Senate club, which always protects its own, prevailed," DeMint wrote.) The result, says Bennett, was that "every member of the conference comes out furious at DeMint and completely supportive of Mitch." As Bennett concludes: "That's the way Mitch gets to be leader and maintains people's respect and backing. . . . No one remembers that it was his proposal that wasn't adopted—they just remember that DeMint was a real pain—and Mitch came out unscathed."

McConnell was unscathed within the conference, perhaps, but he was unable to avoid the ultimate consequence of the insurgency. Despite a historic triumph for Republicans in the 2010 midterm election—sixty-three seats gained in the House, plus a surge in state capitals—McConnell came up four votes short of a Senate majority. Almost certainly, he would have achieved his life's goal had the conservative uprising not left the party with fringe candidates in eminently winnable races, in Nevada, Colorado, and Delaware, where the party's nominee took to the airwaves late in the race to address her previous admission to having "dabbled in witchcraft." It was a classic example of blowback: standing by as the party cast Barack Obama as the devil incarnate, and winding up with an ex-sorceress on the Republican ballot.

———

By 2011, the DeMint wing of the Republican caucus had grown larger. Privately, McConnell was losing his patience with them. As one longtime associate of his recalls, McConnell cut loose once in the associate's presence: "He said, 'Those idiots, those people come up here and have never been in office and know nothing about being in office. . . . They don't sit and learn, they just decide they're going to take away every law that's been on the books for fifty years. They want to create chaos—and it worries me a lot.'"

Indeed, chaos arrived halfway into 2011, in the form of the refusal by congressional Republicans to raise the nation's debt ceiling in the absence of deep spending cuts, thus hastening the possibility of a market-shaking credit default. But if McConnell worried about that chaos, he didn't let on—for weeks he deferred to the Republican House leaders driving the confrontation with Obama. When he did speak out, it was to express hope that a deal could be reached—not for the sake of the economy, but to deprive Democrats of a campaign talking point: "If we go into default, [Obama] will say that Republicans are making the economy worse," he said. "All of a sudden we have co-ownership of a bad economy. . . . That is very bad positioning going into an election."

Only in the final moments did McConnell help negotiate a deal that infuriated many Democrats—no new tax revenues and the threat of big future spending cuts. With the crisis averted, McConnell seemed to gloat about the episode, casting it as a clever use of leverage. "I think some of our members may have thought the default issue was a hostage you might take a chance at shooting," he told the *Washington Post*. "Most of us didn't think that. What we did learn is this—it's a hostage that's worth ransoming." He promised that when it came time for another debt ceiling increase a few years later, "we'll be doing it all over."

That was hardly the sort of language that was going to restrain the hostage takers McConnell was privately criticizing. And they were not about to be restrained. In the spring of 2012, they claimed another of his few confidants in the Senate—Richard Lugar, who had done McConnell the favor of renominating him as leader just a few years earlier. McConnell had, more recently, been keeping his distance from Lugar, who noticed that McConnell had not exactly been jumping up to support him in his push in 2010 and early 2011 to get their fellow Republicans to vote for the New START nuclear arms reduction treaty, which Obama was seeking with Russia. "Some of the positions I took were not necessarily ones he wanted to support, and sometimes if he did want to support it, he was very quiet about it," says Lugar. That was the case with New START, which McConnell barely mentioned at the caucus's weekly luncheons. "I understood where he was," says Lugar, "and that I had to go about getting the votes on my own."

McConnell was more willing to lend Lugar assistance behind the scenes, as he urged his friend to play rough with his primary opponent, state treasurer Richard Mourdock. Lugar was reluctant to take the advice. "Hitting hard has usually been very effective for Mitch, and he's found it to be so effective that he's been impatient with others who . . . are not willing to sock it to somebody," says Lugar. "He knew I was working hard at [the campaign] but was not being supercritical [of Mourdock] and he'd say, 'You really have to sock it to him.'" Lugar chose not to do so, and was overwhelmed by the same archconservative anger as Bob Bennett had been, losing by 20 percentage points. McConnell was open with Lugar about who was to blame: the outside groups whipping up a frenzy on the party's far fringe. "In private conversation, he very well understood what was happening with Freedom Works and

Club for Growth and the Koch brothers and whoever else you wanted to talk about," Lugar says. But hadn't McConnell spurred that wave in his own right with his whole approach to the Obama presidency? "Mitch has been so successful that I'm not going to argue with it," Lugar says.

By McConnell's own terms, he hadn't been successful: that November, Obama was elected to a second term—and Republicans were left with two fewer seats in the Senate, including Lugar's. Rather than preparing for a Republican administration, McConnell was left reckoning with another precipice created by the brinkmanship his anti-Obama strategy had encouraged, the "fiscal cliff" the country was facing at end of 2012 with the expiration of the Bush tax cuts, and the arrival of the deep sequestration cuts that had been part of the 2011 debt-ceiling deal. With his talks stalling with his Democratic counterpart, Harry Reid, McConnell called up Vice President Joe Biden, his longtime Senate colleague. "Does anyone down there know how to make a deal?" he demanded to know. He and Biden hashed out a deal that, once again, upset many Democrats—making permanent the Bush tax cuts for all income under $400,000, a far higher threshold than Obama wanted, and delaying the spending cuts by only two months. "You could argue persuasively, that—in a government controlled two-thirds by the Democrats—we got permanency for ninety-nine percent of the Bush tax cuts," McConnell said in persuading his fellow Republicans to vote for the package, according to the *Washington Post*.

Those who benefited from McConnell's preservation of so many upper-end tax cuts did not need persuading. Back in Kentucky, McConnell won great gratitude from the likes of Bill Stone, the owner of a large glass manufacturer in Louisville and former chairman of the Jefferson County GOP. Stone especially appreciated that the deal had prevented a big increase in the estate tax— the tax-free exemption stayed above $5 million, and the top rate went to 40 percent, far less than the exemption of only $1 million and rate of 55 percent that would have gone into effect without the deal. "Mitch is a hero—every small businessman and farmer with a ranch who's got a small fortune ought to kiss his feet," Stone says. As soon as the deal was struck, a tired McConnell got on a plane to New Orleans for the Sugar Bowl, where Louisville was playing Florida. Waiting for him was Stone, who thanked McConnell for his work keeping the estate tax in check. "Mitch staggered into a brunch with the president of Louisville and dropped into a chair and said, 'Bill, given the position we were in, we did the absolute best we could,'" Stone recalls. Stone assured McConnell that he had done more than enough. "I got to be the one that thanked him. He gave that smile of understanding, that knowing smile."

McConnell's success in closing the deals on the debt-ceiling crisis and fiscal cliff was a reminder of his skill as a negotiator. (Chris Dodd jokes that working with McConnell on the 2002 bill to repair the country's broken voting system put him in mind of Egyptian president Anwar Sadat's line that negotiating his peace deal with Israeli prime minister Menachem Begin was the "most dreadful and most beautiful thing I ever did." McConnell, Dodd says, is "the toughest guy—every article, semicolon is a wrestling match, and that was the dreadful thing. When I was done I slept like a baby because I knew it was golden—I knew it was going to happen. . . . Every penny of that four billion dollars got through the appropriators.") But the deals also pointed to the way in which McConnell was learning to capitalize on the Tea Party element within his caucus that he privately deplored. After all, his bargaining hand was strengthened by that faction's extremism, its willingness to press its case to the point of threatening real harm to the national and world economy—with Republicans so willing to risk a credit default in 2011, the White House had had to settle for a deal in which it got almost nothing it wanted except for being spared a credit default. If McConnell was not doing more outwardly to restrain the far wing of his party and his caucus, even now that the goal of preventing a second Obama term had been dashed, this dynamic was perhaps one reason why.

As unrealistic as their demands were, the insurgents were an effective weapon in his showdowns with the administration he had set out to defeat.

It was hard to see how even McConnell was supposed to capitalize on the next showdown, the government shutdown forced by congressional Republicans' insistence on defunding the Patient Protection and Affordable Care Act, aka "Obamacare." McConnell made no secret that he found the gambit foolhardy, but instead of trying to quash it, he absented himself even more than he had done in the early stages of the prior crises. His most notable appearance, as the shutdown ticked on and eight hundred thousand federal workers were furloughed, was a private exchange with Rand Paul, picked up on a hot mike, in which the two discussed the shutdown in purely partisan, tactical terms: "We're gonna win this, I think," said Paul. Predictably, McConnell once again made his last-minute arrival to negotiate a conclusion to the shutdown with Harry Reid.

As Judd Gregg, McConnell's former ally in the Senate, sees it, McConnell's handling of the shutdown episode exposed his caucus's archconservatives, such as Texas's Ted Cruz, for the self-aggrandizing extremists they were, without requiring a confrontation by McConnell (DeMint himself had already departed for a high-paying job running the Heritage Foundation, which, awkwardly enough, was also where Elaine Chao was now installed). "He handled it in true Mitch style—give them enough rope so they self-destruct," Gregg says, embarking on a mixed-metaphor riff. "Mitch gave them the running room to do what they needed to do. It's Mitch's management style—he lets the cards play out until he plays his cards and then he wins. . . . It would've been whistling in the wind to step in at an earlier point."

Perhaps so—but McConnell's "win" had come at a major cost, not least what economists estimated was the shutdown's $24 billion setback for the national economy. It's not hard to imagine another approach by McConnell in handling his caucus's right wing, says Merkley, the Oregon Democrat: "There was no apparent effort by senior leaders . . . to convey the destructive nature of this paralysis . . . to pull in members who had come here with 'Government is the enemy and we're going to melt down the Senate as part of hatred of the government,'" he says. "It would have taken senior members to say, 'That doesn't work here. We are here with a constitutional responsibility and we have an obligation to address the issues and are not going to tolerate folks unilaterally melting this place down.'"

Far from it. Post-shutdown, McConnell showed no sign of a break in approach. In what Reid called a "breach of faith" with an informal earlier agreement to let more nominations through, McConnell led his caucus to block three of Obama's nominees for the influential D.C. Circuit Court of Appeals, to keep the president from tilting the court's ideological direction, just as he had led a filibuster of Obama's nominee to lead the new Consumer Finance Protection Bureau to keep that agency, a creation of the financial-reform law, from functioning.

As always, McConnell and his closest allies in the Senate argued that these tactics were only ripostes to Reid's domineering ways, notably his limitation on Republicans' ability to offer amendments on bills. Democrats, of course, countered that it was the Republicans' predilection since 2007 for troublemaking amendments and for the filibuster that had forced Reid's hand. "It's a question of chicken and the egg, and to me it's abundantly clear what came first. What came first is Republicans using the filibuster," says Conrad, the former senator from North Dakota. Norman Ornstein, the congressional scholar at the American Enterprise Institute, says there is simply no question who had done the most to explode long-standing norms. Under McConnell, he says, Republicans had regularly used filibusters on motions to proceed, not just on legislation, and had insisted, after a successful sixty-person vote for cloture, to use the full thirty hours allotted for debate—not to actually debate, but simply to chew up time. Yes, Reid was limiting amendments, but even that rationale for obstructionism fell away when it came to using the filibuster and "blue slips" to block lower-level administration nominees and federal judges. "The use of the filibuster to deny the president his team, or to block judges when there were no real quibbles about qualifications or ideology, is a major breach of Senate norms, and Mitch McConnell is responsible," Ornstein wrote in 2014.

Some Republicans seemed to agree: When Merkley tried in late 2012 to coax some Republicans into a deal to limit filibusters, he says the response from several was: "The ideas you're putting forward are reasonable, but there's no way I can be out there . . . out of sync with McConnell and his agenda of paralyzing this place." When McConnell told his fellow Republicans in a closed-door meeting in July 2013 that he could've done better than the deal they negotiated without him to approve some of Obama's nominations, an exasperated Bob Corker, the Tennessee senator, called "bullshit" loud enough for the room to hear, reported *Roll Call*. Ira Shapiro, a former Senate staffer, Clinton administration trade official, and author of a history of the Senate, argued in a May 2014 opinion piece that the Senate would be functioning better with just about any other Republican in McConnell's place. "Virtually every serious observer thinks that the Senate would be a far different place if the Republicans were led by someone else, such as Lamar Alexander, Rob Portman, Susan Collins or Bob Corker," Shapiro wrote.

At one point, McConnell and Reid had enjoyed the modicum of a working relationship. They had in common their affection for Washington's new baseball team, their avoidance of the Beltway social circuit, and their devotion to the Senate, an institution that they, unlike many of the chamber's presidential wannabes, were content to spend their careers in. The breakdown of the Obama years, though, had frayed whatever tenuous bond there had once been. Reid was still smarting over the intensity of the Republican leadership's push against his reelection in 2010 (in one particularly personal attack, the NRSC ran ads ridiculing Reid for staying at a condo unit in the Ritz-Carlton while in Washington). Their meetings on major legislation and the various fiscal crises too often ended with the more blunt Reid having made his position clear but being left with no idea of where the more reserved McConnell stood—McConnell would insist on running everything past his kitchen cabinet and caucus before making a counteroffer. Their regular Monday meetings sputtered to a halt, leaving their brief exchanges on the floor after convening the Senate each day as the extent of their communication. The low point for Reid may have come in June 2012, when, after much haggling to build broad support for a flood insurance bill, Reid brought it to the Senate floor only for Rand Paul to demand to hold it hostage until the Senate allowed a vote on an unrelated "personhood amendment," giving legal protections to fetuses right at fertilization.

Reid's payback gathered over time. In the summer of 2013, a SuperPAC run by his close allies started running ads attacking McConnell, eighteen months before his next election. In September, Reid held a reunion dinner in the Senate for all of the living Senate majority leaders—a category defined to exclude McConnell. The break was made final, though, with Reid's announcement in late 2013 that the Democrats would vote by simple majority to undo the filibuster for most presidential nominations—the oft-threatened "nuclear option" that McConnell had warned would make Reid the "worst Senate leader ever"—and thereby fill long-vacant slots in the judiciary and administration. Republican indignation followed: "The Senate is being destroyed as an institution," says Gregg. In January, McConnell gave a lengthy floor speech deploring what Reid had done to the Senate: "What have we become?" he said. "The Senate seems more like a campaign studio than a serious legislative body. . . . We've gotten too comfortable with doing everything we do here through the prism of the next election, instead of the prism of duty. And everyone suffers as a result."

If there was any self-criticism in this indictment—after all, it was McConnell who had declared in 2010 his overriding goal a partisan victory in the election two years hence—it was hard to discern. He pledged that if Republicans gained the majority the following year, they would do things differently, by reempowering committee chairmen, restoring a robust amendment process, and lengthening the Senate workweek. As the *Washington Post* noted, though, McConnell himself had played a role in each of the tendencies he deplored—he had weakened committee prerogative with his undermining of Baucus's work with Grassley on health care, abetted the use of poison-pill amendments by fellow Republicans, and was himself often skipping out of the Senate early for fund-raisers around town. "McConnell," wrote Ornstein, "is much less a victim and much more a perpetrator."

That last tendency McConnell had mentioned—cutting out early for fund-raisers—was especially strong come early 2014. McConnell was himself, now more than ever, seeing his work through the prism of the next election.

———

The aroma of some twenty thousand pounds of barbecued pork and mutton hung in the midsummer air as Mitch McConnell stepped to the podium beneath the pavilion at Fancy Farm, the annual church-picnic-meets-political-festival hosted yearly by a Catholic parish in rural western Kentucky. In August 2013, it represented the unofficial kickoff to the 2014 campaign season. Fancy Farm is politics at its most archaic and elemental—not only are barbed speeches and raucous audiences permitted, they are demanded.

It is a perennially uncomfortable setting for Mitch McConnell. Dressed on this day in a denim shirt and pleated khakis, he gave it his best—his voice cracked at the outset but rounded into a full growl as he laid into his Democratic opponent, Alison Lundergan Grimes, the young secretary of state and daughter of Kentucky power broker Jerry Lundergan. "How nice it is to see Jerry Lundergan back in the game. Like the loyal Democrat he is, he's taking orders from the Obama campaign on how to run his daughter's campaign," McConnell began, to hollers from the college Republicans in matching red T-shirts, whom his campaign had bused in for the event. From there followed a barrage linking Grimes with faraway liberals conspiring against the Bluegrass State: "We're going to decide what kind of America we're going to have: Barack Obama's vision for America or Kentucky's. You know, I've brought Kentucky's voice to Washington, and the Obama crowd doesn't like it because the Kentucky voice is often the voice of opposition to the Obama agenda. That's why every liberal in America wants to beat us next year. You know, the liberals are worried because just as I predicted Obamacare is a disaster for America. I fought them every step of the way on the government takeover. And we stand up to their war on coal. As long as I'm in the Senate, Kentucky will have a voice instead of San Francisco and Martha's Vineyard. Look, all these liberals coming down here to push me around, they're not going to get away with it, are they? . . ." And on it went.

Grimes dished out plenty when it came her turn—"If the doctors told Senator McConnell he had a kidney stone, he would refuse to pass it," she said. She offset her pugilistic speech with her move, in a detour from her way back to her seat, to greet McConnell and Elaine Chao with a big smile. McConnell, caught off guard, stayed frozen in his seat and stared at Grimes while his wife jumped up for a handshake.

But Grimes wasn't McConnell's real concern that day. His confidence in regards to his Democratic opposition was on display a few months earlier, when it looked as if he might be facing Ashley Judd, the Kentucky-bred Hollywood actress turned liberal activist. "When anybody sticks their head up, do them out," McConnell said in a secretly recorded meeting where he and his aides discussed possible attack targets for Judd (her admission to considering suicide in sixth grade was one). No, McConnell's real concern early in the campaign, as it had been for the past few years in Washington, was about keeping abreast of his party's rightward lurch, which now meant fending off a conservative challenger, a wealthy businessman and Tea Party acolyte named Matt Bevin. So McConnell had locked down an early endorsement from Rand Paul—a gesture as expedient as could be expected between the man who had introduced the 2007 legislation that loosened restrictions on National Security Agency eavesdropping and the man who had staged a thirteen-hour filibuster over the threat of surveillance drones. Asked by a constituent in Edmonton, Kentucky, in April why he had endorsed McConnell, Paul "declined to answer the question publicly," the *Glasgow Daily Times* reported, "saying he would speak with her in private and explain his reason for supporting the senior senator."

To secure Paul's support, McConnell had joined Paul's filibuster of the nominee for the CIA and his bill to cut off military aid for Egypt and even taken up a pet cause of Paul's and many of his Kentucky followers: the legalization of hemp. Most conspicuously, McConnell hired as his campaign manager Jesse Benton, the husband of Paul's niece and the manager of Paul's general election campaign in 2010. Benton, so youthful that he was barely indistinguishable from the students at Fancy Farm whom he was leading in cheers and jeers that afternoon, let it be known just how expedient his new role was when he told a conservative activist, in a call that was taped and later released, that "I'm sorta holding my nose for two years" to work for McConnell. McConnell, in turn, confirmed the transactional nature of the arrangement when he opted to keep Benton in the job despite this remark. The team led by the Tea Party consultant, Benton, set about savaging the Tea Party candidate, Bevin, by, among other things, putting out an ad charging that he had falsely claimed a degree from the Massachusetts Institute of Technology—a charge based on a stray mention on a LinkedIn page.

It was a formidable show of force on McConnell's right flank, but its intensity revealed the odd reality of his position in Kentucky. For someone who had represented the state in the Senate for three decades, his standing was shaky. Somehow, over all that time, he had failed to build up the residual goodwill that most veteran politicians accrue simply by showing up, reaching out, and spreading favors. It wasn't for lack of trying. In the glory days of congressional earmarks, before Congress curtailed them in 2011, McConnell had snared dollars for his state with the best of them: $38 million for a parks venture in suburban Louisville led by the CEO of Humana, the giant health insurer based in Louisville, a top McConnell donor; millions for the Land Between the Lakes recreational area in western Kentucky; $199,000 for "beaver control" in Kentucky. "My definition of pork is a project in Indiana," he once quipped. Many of the earmarks ended up with his name attached to them: money for the Mitch McConnell Park in Bowling Green, the Mitch McConnell Plaza and Walkway in Owensboro, the Mitch McConnell Integrated Applications Laboratory at Western Kentucky University, the Mitch McConnell Center for Distance Learning at the University of Kentucky. "He's quite adept at building monuments to himself," says Hollenbach, his first opponent. "Everything he brought back was to memorialize or perpetuate his name."

McConnell had played a part in crafting the $10 billion buyout to compensate tobacco growers for the end of price supports for the crop. He had helped set up a compensation fund and cancer screening program for workers exposed to plutonium at the big uranium-enrichment plant in Paducah, albeit only after longstanding concerns about the plant became a national story. His plying of his constituents' attention extended to his diligence about staying visible back home. He made a point of doing his own grocery shopping at the Kroger near his house, and could be spotted at University of Louisville football games.

But the affection didn't follow—far from it. McConnell found himself the subject of nationwide ridicule for an ad his campaign posted online in March showing him looking even more bloodless than usual. "Nobody in the state loves him—hell, his friends don't love him. It's not about love," says Jim Cauley, the consultant who worked on Sloane's and Beshear's challenges. McConnell's success at mastering the institution he loved in the city he'd been so eager to flee to as a young man had left a sense of distance between him and his constituents. In a state with a strong populist streak, no number of sightings in the soda aisle could repair this estrangement. (It didn't help that his and Chao's net worth was now up to somewhere between $9.2 million and $36.5 million, according to his finance closure statements—an astonishing sum for a man who had spent barely any time working in the private sector.) "He can't connect with anybody here," says Mark Guilfoyle, a northern Kentucky lawyer who served as general counsel to one of the state's former Democratic governors. "He's inside the Beltway—you just listen to him talk about all these arcane rules of the Senate . . . and it puts you to sleep. Mitch McConnell is an elite, end of story— and they don't play well in Kentucky."

Recognizing this reality, McConnell had all but stopped seeking his state's love and had taken up a line that tried to turn the distance to his advantage: a state so removed from the nation's power structure should count itself lucky to have one of its own at the table when the big decisions are being made. "You can't get any of those things done from the back bench," he said in his Fancy Farm speech. Touting his role in the deal to end the government shutdown, he said: "I've demonstrated, once again, that when the Congress is in gridlock and the country is at risk, I'm the guy who steps forward and tries to get us out of the ditch." It was as persuasive an argument as McConnell could hope to make, says Al Cross, the former political writer for the *Courier-Journal*. "Kentuckians have an inferiority complex—we know we lag behind other states for so many things," says Cross. As a result, the state's voters "are glad to have a Kentuckian in a position of power—not just to bring home the bacon, but to make Kentucky look better."

The rest of the campaign followed in the lockstep McConnell had adopted for some time now. In March, he came onto the stage at CPAC, the big convention of conservative activists in Washington, gripping a rifle in his right hand. He railed against the new health-care law, even as it flourished in his state, covering more than four hundred thousand Kentuckians thanks to the enthusiastic implementation by Beshear, now the state's governor. (McConnell eventually wound himself into knots trying to argue that the law's benefits for Kentucky were separate from the Obamacare he wanted to repeal.) He led the way in the Senate in blocking Democratic efforts on an array of measures—extended benefits for the unemployed, increases in the minimum wage, funding for veterans' health care. He led a filibuster on one bill, a bipartisan series of energy-efficiency measures, only to deny an accomplishment for the Democratic senator from New Hampshire who was facing a competitive reelection campaign that could determine the Senate majority. He sought revenge for Reid's elimination of the filibuster for presidential nominations the previous fall by leading Republicans in stalling, by other procedural tactics, so many uncontroversial nominations that by August 2014 a backlog of more than a hundred had developed, including ambassadorships to the highly relevant posts of Russia and Turkey.

He was as locked into his partisan warrior mode as ever before: when, on one occasion, he encountered John Yarmuth, the former colleague turned Democratic congressman whom he has since broken sharply with, at the VIP lounge at Reagan National Airport, he did not greet him. "He was staring straight at me as I walked in, and no one else was there except his security people," says Yarmuth. "He looked at me and there was not a muscle in his face that moved."

Bevin's campaign fizzled in the homestretch, beset by a lack of finances (he got some help from a conservative group founded by McConnell's nemesis DeMint, but many others who preferred him lacked assurance he had enough of a shot at beating McConnell for them to risk incurring McConnell's ire). McConnell refused to debate Bevin, depriving him of an opportunity to confront

McConnell directly. The revelation that Bevin had signed a 2008 investment report praising that year's financial bailout deprived him of the ideological purity claimed by the little-known economics professor who would upset House majority leader Eric Cantor in June. There were also distractions like the report of Bevin's attendance at a pro-cockfighting rally. On May 20, McConnell beat Bevin by 24 percentage points—a margin so wide that one couldn't help but think back to all the rightward tacking that had been undertaken, all for the sake of countering an underfunded challenger left to seek votes from aggrieved cockfighters.

This victory left Grimes, McConnell's Democratic opponent. She had improved as a candidate and was quite deft at attacking McConnell—she criticized him for governing "out of spite" and "acting petty and small" and compared him unfavorably in this regard with the great senators of Kentucky past. But she still could appear stilted and overprogrammed, particularly when discussing her party's agenda in Washington. ("She has an odd way about how she comes across," says Ted Jackson, a top Republican strategist in Kentucky who backs McConnell. "She has hollow eyes. . . . I'm not saying she's stupid, but she doesn't look prepared. She just has that look—her eyes kind of pop out at you.") She had raised impressive amounts of money, but was short of McConnell's $10.4 million pile, which was just waiting to be deployed against an untested challenger in a state that had gone Republican by 22 points in the 2012 election. A betting man would still go with Mitch McConnell winning his sixth term, and, along with that, achieving his life's dream of being Senate majority leader.

Which would then raise an important question: Once in that high position, what would McConnell seek to do with it? What, really, had been his purpose all along?

———

In the lower level of the University of Louisville library a visitor finds a curious display in the large anteroom to the Senator Mitch

McConnell and Secretary Elaine L. Chao Archives. Opened in 2009, with a Ronald Reagan quote about freedom emblazoned on its entrance, the "Civic Education Gallery" is a shrine to McConnell and, secondarily, his second wife. (Unmentioned is his first wife, Sherrill, who ended up in western Massachusetts, overseeing a women's history archive at Smith College. Speakers at her 2013 retirement party included Gloria Steinem; Alison Bechdel, the author of the syndicated comic strip *Dykes to Watch Out For;* an advocate for mothers in prison; a Native American rights activist; and the former black nationalist leader of a rape-crisis center.)

The basement gallery is an unusual memorialization for an elected official still in the fray. But then, Mitch McConnell has long had an eye on his place in history—there are the lengthy oral history interviews he's been giving for years now to the Kentucky historian, John Kleber. And there is the big portrait he sat for, on his parents' dime, in 1984—the year he was first elected to the Senate. It hangs in a second, smaller display upstairs in the library.

What is most striking about the gallery is not its mere presence but how McConnell has chosen to celebrate his career. There are some mementoes from his youth—his baseball glove, the RCA Victor radio that he and his father followed sports on, the honorary paddle from his fraternity, Phi Kappa Tau. But when it comes to his actual political career, the overriding focus of the gallery is not on McConnell's achievements while in office in Louisville and Washington, but on the elections that got him into those positions. There are framed newspaper front pages from each of McConnell's victories. There are video clips of his campaign ads—and even a small sculpture given to him by an admirer depicting the hound-dog ad used against Huddleston. There is a photograph from a 1986 McConnell fund-raiser attended by Vice President Bush: the caption announces it "broke all previous Kentucky records."

The gallery's focus on McConnell's electoral successes is true to the man. Those who have worked alongside McConnell, friends and rivals alike, struggle to identify the governing purpose that has motivated him throughout decades of exertion in the public sphere. "I don't have the vaguest idea," says Chris Dodd, who spent a quarter century alongside McConnell in the Senate and who was once invited to give a lecture at the McConnell Center in Louisville.

What has motivated McConnell has not been a particular vision for the government or the country, but the game of politics and career advancement in its own right. "It's to win and have power," says Harvey Sloane, McConnell's 1990 opponent.

"He literally eats and sleeps and digests politics every hour," says Lance Tarrance, the pollster for McConnell's first Senate campaign. "I don't think I ever met anyone who was so hardwired for politics."

"He's playing the game," says Brian Atwood, the former USAID administrator who faced off against McConnell over foreign aid budgets. "He's doing it for himself and his game."

Politics "is his avocation, vacation, vocation, all three," says Alan Simpson, the former Republican senator from Wyoming.

"I don't think he stands for anything. Politics is sport to him. It's how he lives," says Frank Greer, who managed Sloane's 1990 campaign.

"He's like Bobby Fischer," says Bruce Lunsford, McConnell's 2008 opponent. "Fisher could only do chess—he was so socially inept, he couldn't do anything else. That's what Mitch is like."

"It's always been about power, the political game, and it's never been about the core values that drive political life," says John Yarmuth, the Democratic congressman from Louisville who used to work with McConnell. "There has never been anything that interested him other than winning elections."

"What drives him is absolute dedication to political activity," says Larry Forgy, Reagan's Kentucky campaign chairman. "If he was not elected he would be like a TB victim when you remove the oxygen—it's what feeds him."

Love for the sport of politics is embedded in our nation's fabric and integral to any well-functioning democracy—it is what helped give rise to the press in the new America, it is what helped make nominating conventions such great theater, and it is what helps sustain many unpaid and underpaid campaign foot soldiers toiling long hours for their party's side. But in its extreme form, shorn of principles or convictions, the political game becomes a hollow endeavor, barely less meaningless or self-interested than the competition on display in a smoke-filled off-track betting parlor.

The political culture of the nation's capital has been overtaken by this way of thinking. Newly elected House members on Capitol Hill have barely arrived in Washington when party elders instruct them to start doing "call time" to raise money for their reelection two years hence. Party leaders announce early in midterm election years or even late the year before that no legislation carrying the potential for strife or controversy will be considered until the election—at which the point the cycle of deferral soon begins again. Much of the capital's commentariat, meanwhile, is more than satisfied with this state of affairs: elections are, after all, more entertaining to cover than drawn-out legislative morasses. They make it possible to declare winners and losers without having to weigh policy particulars or worry about being accused of partisan favoritism. As the Beltway has become increasingly prosperous and removed from the rest of the country, it has become more acceptable for elected officials to fixate on doing whatever they must to remain there.

And no one in Washington embodies this prevailing mind-set more than Mitch McConnell. It is he who, with his ardent defense of the flow of big money into campaigns, has helped make it so incumbent on elected officials and challengers alike to obsess about their fund-raising accounts long before the proper campaign season. It is he who has demonstrated the power that can accrue to those who simply guard their rank in their party, wherever the party may lead them. And it is he who, with that one declaration elevating above all the defeat of Barack Obama, articulated the ethos

of the permanent campaign as no one else could. "When he came
out and said his number-one priority was not solving the problems
of the country but that his number-one priority was defeating the
president, that crossed the line for me," says Kent Conrad, the
retired Democratic senator from North Dakota. "Partisans have to
understand there is a limit to partisanship and in that statement he
completely lost perspective. . . . I mean, my goodness, *that's* your
top priority?"

There was once a time when McConnell had held up models
for a different approach to public service. The display in the university library basement plays up his early bond with John Sherman
Cooper, whose portrait still hangs in McConnell's Senate office. A
touchscreen scroll through McConnell's career quotes him saying
that Cooper was "the first great man I ever met." A wall promi-
nently carries this quote from McConnell: "Senator Cooper taught
me to remain true to my convictions, and to remember that there
are times when you follow and times when you lead. I've never
forgotten that." And a TV ad from McConnell's first campaign, for
Jefferson County executive, includes a shot of his father saying,
"Mitch got a lot from John Sherman Cooper. I think if he was like
that, his mother and I would be very pleased."

McConnell has not been like that. Where Cooper retired
from the Senate after his second full term—and then shot an ad
for McConnell's run for county executive, declaring, in a dig at
the incumbent, that two terms sufficed for any elected official—
McConnell is now on the verge of stretching his Senate career
into his sixth term. Where Cooper took positions on weighty issues
that put him at odds with many in his party and many of his constituents—on civil rights, Vietnam, and much else—McConnell
has, by his own admission, been forever attuned to his self-preser-
vation within his party and state.

In his sessions with Dyche and Kleber, McConnell attempted
to claim the Cooper mantle, suggesting that his rightward turn was
in its own way following the Cooper example: "I could have been a

John Sherman Cooper Republican and been praised by the *Courier-Journal* and *Herald-Leader*. That would have been a much easier path to take for me, but that would have, frankly, not been consistent with my convictions, so I have chosen to do it the hard way."

This claim is as disingenuous as it gets. Yes, McConnell's rightward shift cost him the approval of local liberal elites that he enjoyed when entering politics in Louisville. Shortly before his death in 2006, Barry Bingham Jr., the former publisher of the *Courier-Journal*, declared to a former colleague that "the worst mistake we ever made was endorsing Mitch McConnell."

But the shift had also, by McConnell's own candid admission, made it much easier for him to win elections in an increasingly Republican-leaning state, and to rise within his increasingly conservative party. In moving rightward with his party, he surrendered himself to the current, rather than fighting against it. The capable young moderate who in his early years governed in the mold of Cooper might have opted to serve as an anchor as his party began to drift. With his historical perspective and political instincts, he might have saved the GOP from the fate that Geoffrey Kabaservice, the historian, describes for today's Republicans: a dysfunctional party that is "in the process of shucking off most of its history and heritage," with leaders who show "little interest in appealing to moderates, repudiating extremism, reaching out to new constituencies, or upholding the party's legacy of civil rights and civil liberties," leaving "little likelihood that the GOP would take the lead in working toward bipartisan solutions to the economic crisis or present itself as an effective governing party."

More broadly, with his deep understanding of the Senate, McConnell could have recognized how destructive the realignment of the parties into ideologically cohesive units (especially on the right) would be for a constitutional system that, with its multiple channels for obstruction, had not been designed with such a stark partisan divide in mind. That realignment was being driven by historical forces greater than any one politician, but with his grasp of the institution's dynamics he could have sought ways to mitigate the consequences and prevent the federal government from falling into utter dysfunction.

Endeavoring to avert these fates for his party and the Senate might have ended McConnell's Senate career short of its fourth decade. But it might also have produced the sort of greatness that the library display seeks to conjure through sheer artifice.

McConnell chose otherwise. Staying in Washington became an end in its own right, justifying accommodations on just about every issue short of causing an outright global financial collapse. Having chosen as his animating issue the preservation of politicians' ability to raise enormous sums of money, rather than a cause rooted in the needs of his country and constituents, there was little ballast with which to counter the latest upsurge of the right-wing anger Cooper had pushed against years earlier. If anything, McConnell's fight to preserve the flow of big money in politics had intensified that corrosive anger by fueling the sense among Americans that government had been corrupted by deep-pocketed special interests.

Cooper was alive to witness only the first few years of his younger admirer's drift—he died in 1991. But the other moderate Republican senator with whom McConnell spent even more of his formative years, Marlow Cook, is with us, living in Sarasota, Florida. Cook still follows Washington, and has been discouraged by what's become of McConnell. "Mitch is one of the sharpest politicians that the state of Kentucky has ever seen," he says. "He's smart and he is wise. But I think he is far more interested in election success within the Republican Party than in whether or not we should insure fifty million people who have no insurance or funds to have insurance for themselves. . . . What he's done with his life is become a United States senator. He has shown his political capacity . . . but if you gave him grades for political activity and grades for legislative activity, certainly the first would be by far the greatest accomplishment."

Cook stops short of saying whether he wants to see his former aide elected to his sixth term. "That's the prerogative of the people of Kentucky," he says. "They will make that decision. And we will all be anxiously looking forward to seeing what the result was."

But in one sense, the outcome has already been determined. At some point along the way, Mitch McConnell decided that his own longevity in Washington trumped all—that he would even be willing to feed the public's disillusionment with its elected leaders if it would increase his and his party's odds of success at the polls. That he has come as close as he has to achieving his life's dream of becoming the master of the Senate while surveys show Americans more despairing of their own government than ever before suggests his insidious strategy worked. In the contest of cynical striving versus earnest service, Mitch McConnell already won.

CODA: VICTORY

The dream had been deferred for years, but when it was finally realized, how splendid it was. On November 4, 2014, McConnell trounced Alison Lundergan Grimes, winning by more than 15 percentage points, the second largest of all his reelection margins. He won just about the entire state outside of Louisville and Lexington—in Martin County, where the effects of the 2000 coal slurry spill live on, he won 74 percent of the vote. Barely had he received word of his own victory than news of the broader triumph arrived: Republicans were winning across the country, giving the party more than enough seats in the Senate to finally claim the majority with McConnell at the helm. "Tomorrow, the papers will say I won this race, but the truth is, tonight we begin another race . . . that's the race to turn the country around," he said in his victory speech at a hotel in the suburbs of Louisville—in Jefferson County, where he had celebrated his first victory thirty-seven years earlier.

The midterm election of 2014 had been, in a sense, the perfect Mitch McConnell election. It had been dominated, more than any cycle before it, by the dark money made possible by the court rulings championed by McConnell and by his blockage of legislation to require disclosure of the spending. Groups that did not disclose where their money came from spent more than $215 million, up by more than a third from the 2010 midterm election. More than two-thirds of this undisclosed spending was on behalf of Republicans, according to the Center for Responsive Politics.

McConnell himself benefited hugely from this dark money in his race against Grimes. He received $23 million from outside groups, more than double what Grimes did. Some of the spending was from known entities like the National Rifle Association, but the single biggest outside spender was a mysterious group called the Kentucky Opportunity Coalition, which spent more than $7.5 million on ads attacking Grimes. Because the organization classified itself as a group engaged in "social welfare," not just elections, it did not need to disclose its donors. But its purpose was plain: the only name associated with the group was a veteran of McConnell's prior two campaigns.

The election also suited McConnell in being even more devoid of substantive policy debates than is the norm for modern campaigns, freeing him from having to state what he believed on important issues of the day. McConnell struggled mightily on the few occasions when the subject turned to the success of the Affordable Care Act in Kentucky, where the gains in health coverage had been among the three largest in the country. In the campaign's sole debate, he suggested that the state's version of the law could continue in some form even if the federal law was repealed. The moderator declined to follow up, Grimes failed to challenge the claim nearly as aggressively as she could have, and in the days following it received far less attention than her refusal to say whether she had voted for Obama for president. As John Yarmuth, the Democratic congressman from Louisville who has known McConnell for years, put it in an interview with *The Atlantic* just before the election: "Margaret Mead once said that the only thing worth doing is to add to the sum of accurate information in the world, and Mitch doesn't do a lot of that, especially when it comes to the Affordable Care Act."

If the election had a theme, it was sourness—the sourness that Americans felt about an economy that was improving by many metrics but not enough for them to feel it themselves, and the sourness they felt about a government in Washington that seemed disconnected from their anxieties and was getting nothing done. Just as McConnell had calculated it would, this sourness rebounded against the party holding the White House, never mind who had engineered the standstill. And that fallout would now elevate him to the post he had aspired to for most of his life.

Given the nature of McConnell's strategy, it was jarring to hear him declare in his victory speech at the suburban Louisville Marriott that he hoped that, with him in charge of the Senate, Democrats and Republicans could start working together once again. "Just because we have a two-party system doesn't mean we have to be in perpetual conflict," he said.

As brazen as this pivot toward comity might have seemed, it was not out of the realm of possibility that McConnell actually hoped to reach consensus on a few issues. As always, everything was about the next election, but the calculus around the next election might have changed now that his party was in the majority: where before it had helped his side to stymie the president, since the blame would accrue mainly to him, now the electoral consequences of dysfunction might also fall on a Congress under Republican control. Cooperation might now be in his self-interest.

There was, of course, another possible motivation for trying to accomplish some things in Washington, as Yarmuth noted in his *Atlantic* interview. Just moments earlier, Yarmuth had been telling a pro-Grimes rally that McConnell "doesn't have any core values. He just wants to be something. He doesn't want to do anything." But now he noted that McConnell might just want to do something for the sake of his place in the annals of the institution he revered. "If he were to become majority leader, I think he actually will try to make things better," Yarmuth said. "He will begin to think about his legacy, and he will not want the history books to write how he has been for the last thirty years."

If so, it would be a long time in coming. But it would, in all likelihood, be too late.

ABOUT THE AUTHOR

Alec MacGillis is a senior editor at *The New Republic*. He previously covered national politics and domestic policy for *The Washington Post* and worked as a reporter at the *Baltimore Sun* and *Concord Monitor* in New Hampshire, among other papers. A native of Pittsfield, Massachusetts, he now resides with his family in Baltimore.

Get email updates on

ALEC MACGILLIS,

exclusive offers,

and other great book recommendations

from Simon & Schuster.

Visit **newsletters.simonandschuster.com**

or

scan below to sign up: